WILUMINA AND THE WELL

JENNIFER DAWN MADDOX

Printed in the United States of America

First Printing, 2023
ISBN 979-8-9895774-1-5

PRAISE FOR *WILUMINA AND THE WELL*

"*Wilumina and the Well had a deep resonance with my soul. My life will never be the same.*

Wilumina and the Well is a survival guide for trauma recovery and a story of enduring love. I hope that every person who may be feeling lost, scared or alone finds love and courage to heal their own story through the eyes and bravery of Wilumina Florida Pearl."

~ Tererai Trent, PhD, Author of *The Awakened Woman*

"*Wilumina and the Well is a beautiful story of the mystical path of healing. Highly recommended for anyone on a journey of self-love and transformation.*"

~ Dr. Laurel Hicks, PhD

"*Dearest Jennifer, I finished your book. Tears of joy! You covered and conquered the difficult topic of abuse with sensitivity, grace, love, and an abundance of creative exuberance. Anyone who reads your book's incredible hero's story will agree that your courage and wisdom shine through as a guiding light. Brava!*"

~ Charlotte Eulette, poet and co-founder of
the Celebrant Foundation & Institute

"*Beautifully written. It takes you to a magical world inside of yourself and opens you up to compassion and love. It changed the way I feel about myself and my body.*"

~ Molly Murer, Account Manager

"*Wilumina and the Well is a beautiful story of the incredible power of the healing that can happen when we have the courage to face our past trauma with self-compassion and self-love.*"

~ Peace Mitchell, Cofounder of Women Changing the World

"Wilumina and the Well *rocked me to my core. A beautiful masterpiece of the courage it takes to look at our pain. A must read for anyone that needs a helping hand to navigate their journey of healing.*"

~ Katie McDonald, Life Coach

"*A beautifully written story about the magic and struggles of the human heart, deeply connected to Earth and the wonder of spirit.*"

~ Nikoletta Dax, Detox Specialist

"*Sweetly rich and soulfully deep, this heart-opening tale takes us on an epic journey.* Wilumina and the Well *illuminates the complexities of childhood psyche and development and inspired me to look at my own story through a different lens. As the book unfolds, it will transport you to another realm, open your heart and leave you craving more.*"

~ Carrie Diehl, Artist & Educator

Foreword

I met Jennifer shortly after I published my book *The Awakened Woman*. She attended a small weekend workshop I held in New Mexico in 2018. Since then, our relationship has grown into a friendship. At that workshop, when each woman spoke of her dreams, Jennifer spoke about writing a book—this book.

She said to me, "I want to write a book that will tell a story and teach the reader. I want to write the book that I need to read. One about healing, personal growth, and spirituality. Lord knows I need more of all three of those things!"

I said, "Many people have learned from teaching stories or parables for thousands of years. What will your story be about?"

She said she wasn't sure exactly but drew a picture for me of a woman blowing what looked like breath or air across many faces. She handed me the drawing and said, "This."

Looking at the drawing, I didn't quite understand. So, I asked, "What does it mean?"

She answered, "I don't know exactly. But I can feel it, Tererai. It's a story growing in me, and I birthed the idea for it right here with you in New Mexico. Thank you." She went on, "When I complete my book, would you be willing to write the foreword to it?"

I said yes, knowing that she would one day call on me to do just that.

Today is that day! *Wilumina and the Well* is a gem! It reminds me of *A Wrinkle in Time*. The best part of the manuscript is how she cleverly weaves key lessons through the story without being preachy. I foresee this book becoming a staple on every therapist's bookshelf. *Wilumina and the Well* is a survival guide for trauma recovery and a story of enduring love. I hope that every person who may be feeling lost, scared, or alone finds love and courage to heal their own story through the eyes and bravery of Wilumina Florida Pearl.

Jennifer weaves together all the aspects of story, fantasy, and practicality into a tale of a sacred journey. Just like she said she would. I am so honored to write this foreword for Jennifer and to be the woman who inspired the dream of writing *Wilumina and the Well.*

~ Dr. Tererai Trent

Author's Note

I am so happy you have found this life-changing story of *Wilumina and the Well.* Because you have picked up this book and decided to read it, I already know that you are brave. For only the brave are able to really spend time with theirs or anybody else's shadow. And as you will come to learn, the path to the light is through the dark.

There are some scenes in this book that could be triggers for you. I suggest that you have a reading buddy or someone to talk with as you are moving through Wilumina's story. We are not meant to heal in isolation. Perhaps you would like to start a reading group so that you can read this book with a group of people and discuss it along the way? Another suggestion (if you are in therapy) is to ask your therapist, mentor, or adviser to read this book so that they can support you while you are reading. Want to read it solo? That's totally okay too! You might want to have a journal nearby to jot down notes. You might even want to write down questions for your own inner guide for greater insight and answers to some of your own stories.

I have a general resource page at the end of the book. These national US resources are on a larger scale, but they are a good place to start looking for support if you or someone you know is struggling with any of the issues that we will be exploring through Wilumina's adventure.

Mostly, I just want you to know that I am so proud of you that you have gotten to the place where you are today. You are not alone, and you are so much stronger than you give yourself credit for. Keep reading! Keep going even when things get hard. The way to the light is through the dark. It's all sacred, and it's all necessary, and so are you!

There's something magical about wells.

I've always believed that wells hear our wishes.

Even the shopping mall wishing wells have some connection to magic.

They hold our secrets and our desires.

Each person who throws a coin into a well secretly or openly believes the same thing.

It wasn't until I came face-to-face with my special well again that I understood

the true magic a well can perform.

Funny thing is I grew up with a little well in my backyard.

Our little house was across the alley from the church where my dad worked.

I had forgotten…

~ Jennifer Dawn Maddox

Wilumina and the Well

"Lu, I think she's going right now." She was so calm. My sister had been sitting at my mom's bedside for the last thirty days, praying and willing her to wake up from her coma. I had been willing and praying for her to die. My sister had just given the final nod to remove her from the ventilator and feeding tube a few minutes before. The doctors said it would take at least three to seven days for her to pass. My mom had other plans.

I remember, before I left her bedside for the last time, leaning over just like she used to do to me when I was a kid. I whispered in her ear, "Mom, do you want to get out of here?" After the question, I drew back to search her face for answers.

I swear she made a face that said, "Yes!" Her eyes weren't open, but it sure felt like she said, "Yes! Get me out of here!"

I leaned back over her and said, "The only way they're going to let you out of here is if you get up and start eating and talking, or you have to die, and they'll take you out in a body bag." She let out an exhale and fell further into her coma.

It was a horrifying thirty days. Here was this beautiful, complex, amazing soul strapped to her bed because when they unstrapped her, she was violent and thrashed about. Was that her saying, "Get me out of here"? The doctors said it was involuntary muscle responses to her coma and that it was *normal* for coma patients to be tied down. My mom? Tied down? No. She deserved to fly. That was why I wanted her dead.

Now, sitting in my car on the side of the road as I tried to figure out how to get back to her bedside , my sister said those words: "I think she's going right now." We were on the phone confirming my travel plans; my brother was already on his way to her.

I was like, "Wait, what? Now?"

So I shouted to my sister, "Put the phone to her ear! Put the phone to her ear!"

She did, and I could barely hear my mom's rattling breaths over the phone.

I shouted, "I love you, Mom! I love you, Mom! It's okay! You can go!" And then I was silent. As I breathed slowly in and out, calming myself, I listened to my mom's breath slowing, until it stopped. I don't know how long I sat there.

My sister came back on the line and said, "That's it, Lu. She's gone."

Just like that. The greatest force in my life and the giver of my life was gone. I am forever grateful that I got to hear her take her last breaths and be with her in that way as she left this world. In my car, on the side of the road, I closed my eyes, and a strange thing happened. I smiled. My mom was finally at peace. No more fighting, no more demons, just love.

I had a dramatic realization as I opened my eyes. *I'm still here!*

My mom had passed away from this earth, and I was still here! Coupled with my crushing grief I was filled with an overwhelming sense of love, responsibility, and joy for my own life. In the midst of her leaving this world, I came into my own just a little more. Or maybe I had a sense that I understood my life a little more now. I don't remember anything else about the call or even how I got back home for that matter. It was all a blur.

Once I got home, grief took over. I searched for something solid through my tears as grief hijacked my nervous system, setting my body on autopilot. *Get the girls organized. Cry. Go to the grocery store. Cry. Push the shopping cart through the produce aisle.* It didn't matter who might see me crying, and there was no sense in being embarrassed; I was powerless to stop the tears. Through the screen of salt water, I picked out SpaghettiOs, and then back at home, I packed my clothes and kissed my girls goodbye. I got on the airplane through a silent veil of tears. Somewhere I understood that for me to heal, I just needed to let them flow. In my dreams, I heard a distant voice. "Wilumina, my dear, water is the way." Waking up to tears on my pillowcase I became obedient to those tears.

We hadn't planned for her death. She hadn't planned for her death. It came as a storm. It came as an act of desperation for peace and quiet. Her passing didn't come from wanting death but from craving peace. It all went wrong. How was I ever going to live without her? It was so hard living *with* her, but now she was gone.

On the day of her funeral, I felt death gripping me. Even though it was more than three months after her death, and even though I was there with the love and support of my daughters and husband, I felt scared. I felt waves and waves of grief. Her leaving with so many questions unanswered left a gaping hole in my heart and mind.

The funeral took place at the church where I grew up, where my father had proudly served as a youth preacher. The church was across the alley from our little house with the well in the backyard. I hadn't been there in over twenty years. It was a lot to take in.

As her memorial service was ending, I knew I needed to get out of the chapel. I needed to get away from all the guests, all the pomp and circumstance, all the people telling me they were sorry for my loss when they knew neither me nor my mother. My head was pounding, and my spirit wanted to escape. Visitors from my childhood who I never planned on seeing again, men who had molested or assaulted me, people who had been complicit in these crimes, and the old streets and alleyways that held those energies came rushing back in. They brought with them ghosts of the past that I didn't want and couldn't fully recollect. They looked at me with their own wet tears. I felt preyed upon, like these ghostly, hungry souls wanted a piece of me to take with them as a souvenir of my mother's life.

"Oh my, how you look just like her."

Whisperings of suicide…

It was an accident!

One ghost looked me up and down and said, "You are just as beautiful as ever," trying to snake his way into the dominion of my soul. *No! Why are you here? Why are any of you here?*

I could see them salivating at the opportunity to soothe my pain by saying the right thing. Nothing they said was right. It all made me sick. I could feel the saliva rising in the back of my throat. I couldn't spend another second listening to how pretty I looked or how sorry they were. Inside, I was screaming, and my spirit was telling me to fly. I needed to get away. But where could I go? There had been so much flying and fleeing in my life. Where to now? I knew the voice inside telling me to run was my mother's spirit, and I had to answer that calling.

I searched the crowd for an anchor, eyes that loved me. *Marcus, where are you?* Through the crowd, I saw my husband talking with an old woman with wet eyes. He turned, as if he knew I was searching for him. I mouthed, "I have to go."

He made his way over to me and said, "Okay. There's a lot to clean up. It'll keep us busy for at least a few hours. Don't worry, babe. Find a place to lie down. We've got it from here. You've done your part. It was a beautiful eulogy, Lu."

Seeing Marcus and me speaking, my girls stepped away from their chore of collecting the discarded service bulletins from the chapel pews. Sensing my weariness and the concern on Marcus's face, my girls approached gingerly. I told them that I was feeling a little sick and was going to find a place to lie down. I just needed some time alone.

"Okay, Mama," my oldest said. I loved that even though my girls were teenagers, they still called me mama. "We're going to help clean up when everyone leaves. You go rest," she said.

I kissed them all on their foreheads, including Marcus, and whispered, "Thank you." Squeezing Marcus's hand, I turned and started walking to the back of the church. I just needed to breathe for a second and wrestle with this strange sense that my mother was somehow communicating with me. Was it rude of me to go? We had dinner plans in a few hours at a nearby restaurant with all of our extended family. Could I even return? Would I ever want to go back? I couldn't shake the feeling that my mother didn't want me around all those people anymore. She wanted me somewhere else. There was something more important she was pushing me to do.

The little church I grew up in was gone. This church was nothing like I remembered. It had grown and expanded beyond recognition. The grounds, which were once charming, were now a polished maze of manicured walkways and small contemplation gardens. There were arbors and benches dedicated to the church from people long past. The flowers and trees swayed in the breeze. Birds chirped, and insects buzzed. Out of nowhere, images of my mother's discontentment flashed in my mind—breaking glasses at the dinner table, unloading rage on me in my teen years—and it made me momentarily want to tear the neat rows of flowers out of the ground and smash the life out of the birds and insects. This rage came on unexpectedly and without my consent. Perhaps my mother's rage had as well. Was that what she wanted me to know? It didn't feel like that was it. So, I moved on.

The grounds were immense. The once little old church was more like a campus now. They had, in fact, demolished a street so that they could grow and expand the church. They tore down the street where we used to live, way back when I was four or so, when my dad was a youth pastor at this very church. The grounds were now so much bigger, but the construction was still incomplete. There were still more meeting halls to build and rows of plants and trees to be planted.

In a secluded courtyard, I saw a shady spot to sit down. I stopped to look at a beautiful three-tiered fountain with water spouting out the top. The pennies and coins that all the wish seekers had thrown into the wishing well were glistening. I reached in the pocket of my dress and found a solitary coin. I tossed it in and made a wish. It was the wish of all wishes.

What does a daughter wish for at her mother's funeral?

Standing there, I started to cry again; it was the kind of cry that came from the inside of my being, the kind of cry that felt connected to the pain of the earth. I had tried to stay quiet all day, to stay appropriate. But now I couldn't stop it. I fell to the ground right next to the fountain and let my grief flow out of me.

That's when I heard it: "There, there. Let it out."

The voice came from the other side of a construction fence that was plastered with images of the church's new auditorium and other buildings that were coming soon. I got up and went to look over the fence and saw nothing but an abandoned lot with piles of rocks and lots of weeds.

No one was there. I set my foot in the bottom rung of the chain-link and hoisted myself up a little higher to get a better look. Then I set my other foot in another link a bit higher up than the first. A surge of excitement hit me just as a breeze ruffled my skirt. I took a deep breath in and hoisted myself up and over the fence as if it were the most normal thing to do, lifting myself from one world to another. As I walked around, the place felt eerily familiar. Was I a trespasser or a welcomed guest?

The space stretched half the length of the church. It had the sense of something wild. The land was sparse and felt like something used to be there but had been long forgotten. It's interesting how the earth always comes back to claim her place. Was there something I needed to claim as well?

Just then, something unthinkable happened. And even though I was there, it made me question the validity of my memory. Such is the case with people who have experienced trauma—they're not able to recall distinct details of a traumatic event. In that moment, memories began to flood in. Memories that were cloudy and missing context. No real story was present, just feelings and awareness. The patch of land stretched out as long as the church campus. This must have been my old street. The location corresponded to the vision that had formed in my mind. The official name had been Havens Street, but everyone there called it Havens Hollow because of the abundance of trees that sprang up on their own throughout the whole block and its delicate, sloping hollow that looked down to the sea off in the distance. Every house had a tree-filled front and backyard, fed and nourished by a natural underground water source. We lived two houses down from the corner of Havens Street and Saint Anne Street. Looking at it now, there was nothing but scraped earth, rock piles, flowering weeds, and rubble. Every tree was gone. My heart ached for the trees and their powerful network of communication and support for one another—built over decades. Gone, just like that. Nothing but a memory. I followed the slope of scarred earth down to a little spot that was densely populated with some kind of flower and vine. Wild gaggles of flowers exploded through the cracks in the broken pavement, growing where they shouldn't be growing but making a symphony of color, sounds, and smells. They were every-where. They must have been weeds, but to me, they were magnificent!

Life began to show itself. There were bees lightly dancing from one flower to the next. A spider wove an intricate web. There were little birds on the ground gathering seeds and bugs and calling to each other, "Over here! Over here! I found something delicious!" Crickets were chirping and leaping about, and there were a myriad of other creatures and sounds. Was that a frog croaking in the distance? My sadness had settled into my stomach, and I still had the sense I was being called elsewhere. I began to consciously breathe, attempting to let the wildness and beauty of this accidental garden soothe my pain and grief before I moved on.

I took another deep breath in, letting the smell settle into my spirit as I started walking forward between the weeds and flowers. I loved listening to the crunch of the branches and rubble beneath my feet. I continued on, breathing in the perfume of the earth.

The wind picked up, and I felt a swirl of coolness on the back of my neck. It gave me a shiver. I looked around and realized I was alone. There was no one for what seemed like miles, and I didn't care. Alone, I felt the sadness of death and the passing of time weigh on me. But there was still something out there, calling to me. I could smell the salty ocean air off in the distance, and I could feel the coolness as fluffy clouds rolled in from some other distant land across the Pacific. We were about a mile from the ocean. When the onshore winds picked up, Southern California was bathed in the salty, sweet smell of kelp. It smelled like no other. Divine. It mixed with the perfume of the tiny flowers as the wind rustled my hair.

The need to rush fell away from me. I steadied my breath and turned my face toward the sun. I closed my eyes and stood for a few moments, feeling its warmth as the wind stirred. I felt like I was becoming one with the land. It quieted all the other pronouncements of life. Gone were the faces of perpetrators coming to tell me they were "sorry for my loss," with complete disregard for their behavior and what I actually lost. Gone were the thousands of aggravations felt from preparing for my own mother's funeral. I was coming in tune with the landscape that pulsed like a dance of back and forth, of give and take. First were the bees and birds, and now the wind, naturally ebbing and flowing with each other in a dance, swirling together to create a symphony of creation right in the center of complete ruin. The sorrow in my stomach and the waves of grief that passed through me as sobs merged with the rhythms all around me, pulling me in… in… in. Into what? And then I heard something entirely different. Another sound was rising above nature's symphony. What was it?

I moved out of the immediate moment into my head and into my heart and into the rhythm of my blood, which was the rhythm of the waves. I listened with my head, trying to figure out what exactly that sound was. A person? A machine? Then I couldn't hear anything—just blankness. I knew I had at least two hours before anyone would come looking for me. I decided not to worry about the sound and tuned back into my surroundings. I quieted my mind and got in touch with my breath.

Breathe in for a count of five…

Hold for a count of five …

Breathe out for a count of five…

Hold for a count of five …

I did it five times.

I sat down right in the middle of the flowers, bees, crickets, and birds and breathed some more. Deep, cleansing breaths. I had learned from practicing yoga and meditation for many years that the breath is a pathway to peace. Breath is life. The rhythm of the wind is the rhythm of the breath. In and out … in and out. Slow, slow breaths.

Take a deep breath in. One, two, three, four, five …

I reached the top of my breath. *Hold it for one, two, three, four, five.*

I paused and then exhaled, bending forward to really empty out my lungs. There was a rush of oxygen into my system. It took enormous effort to breathe consciously, because in that moment, there was so little place for order, so little place for counting.

"Just breathe deeply and freely," I whispered. "Trust…"

Suddenly my breath was like a roaring ocean raging inside of me, deep breaths flowing like crashing waves. And there it was again—the sounds shaping into words, a little more clearly this time. Was I hearing things? Was someone or something calling me? No, it wasn't my name exactly, but it was a name. A name I thought I'd heard before.

"Luminaaa …" and then *swish* like the sound of air racing through a corridor.

"Luminaaa …"

Swish.

"What is that?" I knew it was not just my imagination. The swish registered in my periphery, not like an image but as a feeling. Like I was surging forward, yet I remained firmly standing on the earth. My name was Wilumina, though most everybody had called me Lu for as long as I could remember.

This word or name seemed to resonate with me as the name of someone I once knew. *Maybe it was me. Curious.* The sound suddenly seemed to be coming from just beyond a pile of rocks covered with weeds and flowers.

"Luminaaa!"

Swish.

I got up and started walking in the direction of the voice. When I started to look around, or when my mind became busy again, the sound dissipated. I stood quietly and breathed. *There it is! Over there now!* Shading my eyes from the sun with my hands, I looked at the center of the next lot over: another pile of rocks covered in flowers and vines. It appeared a little brighter and shinier than the surrounding area. There was a luminescence to it, a certain quality that made it look like it was glowing or the colors were dancing.

A flash of fear entered my system. I was by myself; no one was going to come looking for me anytime soon. What if someone who wanted to harm me was hiding behind that pile of rocks? Was it a trick?

My heart raced as a sudden surge of adrenaline pulsed through my body. I couldn't hear the sound anymore. *Stop. Breathe. Pause.*

There it was… *Swish!*

My body—or the sense of my body—became fractals of light. I expanded and contracted, my cells reverberating like I was expanding and rising and contracting and falling, just for a second.

I heard it again. "Come … safe … here … Luminaaa."

I started walking into the next lot toward the pile of rocks. I saw one remaining tree in the distance at the far end of the lot. Its branches started swaying and dancing as if there was a mighty wind, but the breeze had died down, and the wind had completely stopped. The air was still. Yet the one branch swayed, pointing to the exact area I was walking toward. It seemed to be clapping and dancing all on its own. The symphony of sounds around me quieted down, and though the tree was moving, I couldn't hear its branches.

Time slowed. All the sounds around me stopped. As my footsteps led me, I couldn't help but wonder if it was all in my head. *No, this is a full body experience.*

Swwwisshhhh … whoosh … shhhhhhhhh. The sounds from the branches started up again, getting louder and louder. I was no longer afraid. My heart was pulsating in an unfamiliar way. Then I was running. To where, I wasn't sure; I just knew I was supposed to go.

That's when I saw it. If I hadn't been looking for it, I would not have seen it. But there it was as clear as day: a well. The water spring that was feeding all the magical flowers and weeds was attached to this well!

The sounds were now overwhelming. I dropped to my knees very carefully and with deliberate movement, as if my body knew exactly where to go. *Whoosh* … more sounds, as if I was caught in a tunnel of fractal light, pulling, lifting, expanding, and contracting me at lightning speed. I heard what sounded like laughing, screaming, and primal or ancient rumblings. Then I heard that name again.

"Luminaaaaaaaa."

Upon arrival at the edge of the well, I could see that the mortar between the stones that made up the short wall of the well had collapsed on one side. I went around to the side where it collapsed. The sound was deafening. More screaming and laughter.

What in the world? I had to move rocks out of the way to get close enough to it. I dropped to my hands and knees, moved a rock, and looked into the well. It went deep, deep down into the earth.

At the bottom, it was full of water. It appeared to be just an abandoned well, but holy of all holies, it was more than that. It had to be. Why else were all the sounds coming from it?

Why was it calling me?

"Lu, stop asking questions and just go with this experience," I said to myself.

No one is going to believe this! All the noise around me died down as I began to think. "Breathe," I said.

Then the voice started again. "Lu, come back to this moment. Clear your heart from worry and logic. Take a deep breath in."

I did as I was told.

"That's right. Now blow out the breath and allow yourself to rest into this excitement!"

By taking that breath, the smell of the well filled my lungs. It smelled like life itself. It smelled like the center of the earth. The dark, mossy smell of it combined with those of rock and stone and water and algae and decomposing flora and fauna. It was a deliciously familiar smell. As I peered over the edge of the well and up over the rocky precipice, it seemed bottomless, like it went on forever. But how was that possible?

I could see a reflection of some sort at the very bottom, but I wasn't really sure what I was seeing. Was it a reflection? Was that me? Was that light? I closed my eyes and could still see the light even with my eyes closed. It made no difference. So I opened them again—same thing. I saw the colors and swirls taking shape at the bottom of the well. A sudden explosion of color and light came screaming up through the well.

EEEEEEEEEEEEEAAAAHHHHHH yaaaaaayayayayaya eeeeeeeeee shaaaaaaaa!

The light wave burst onto me, through me, and all around me.

EEEEEEEEEEEEAAAAAAHHHHHHHHH!

Was that me? Was I screaming? Was that sound coming from the well or from inside of me? It was deafening. With it, an enormous wave of vertigo and nausea came over me, along with a strange sense of freedom and release. I turned away from the well and instantly vomited something sour and sweet. It had substance, but it wasn't food. I hadn't eaten since much earlier in the day, and my stomach was empty. Still, I wretched. And as I wretched, colors, patterns, and light swirled around me, gathering momentum. I heard joyous laughter.

On my hands and knees, my back curled and arched with each wave of nausea that hit me like a tsunami of emotions pouring out of me. My back arched as I gasped for air and then curled up as another wave of vomit came and poured out. Stories and tales of pain and poverty washed over me. I began to weep. I cried for myself. I cried for my family. I cried for all the women and children who needed a mother to nurture them and keep them safe.

I cried for the years of self-abuse. I cried for the violence against me and against all women. I cried for the joy and happiness of my children and of my career. I cried for my complicated and loving Marcus. I cried for the trees. I cried for the world and the chaos that it felt. I cried for Mother Earth and for Father Sky. I cried for the years and years I couldn't cry or feel. I cried for the days and weeks I fettered away worrying about anything and everything.

I cried for my mom and for my family and for their pain. I cried for all of the joy and recovery that I was able to create for everyone except myself. I cried for the souls of other dear departed family, friends, and animals.

And my body became wracked in pain. Every joint and every muscle screamed with me. I collapsed near the side of the well. I thought I was going to die. I thought, *Surely this is it. This is the end.* I was dying. My blood felt like shards of glass pulsing through my veins. The glass, ripping and tearing my insides. I was sure blood would flow out of my body soon, yet all I had to offer this pain was tears. I sobbed and huddled on my side, waiting for death.

And then a scream came over me that was from the bottom of the earth and the bottom of the well simultaneously. I screamed the voice of my ancestors. I screamed and wailed like a wild animal. I screamed, howled, cried, and spit. Snot drained out of my nose, tears ran down my face, and vomit poured from me, yet the pain had lifted, and I felt free. Cleansed.

Then I heard it again.

"Luuuummmmiiiinnnaaaa!"

I wiped my face with my sleeve. I took a deep breath in, and with awe and stupor, I crawled back to the well and peered in. The colors were making the shape of a face. I couldn't make it out completely, but it seemed like the face of a beautiful woman. Raven hair swirled around her pale, translucent, and glowing face.

She spoke in a sweet, satiny voice. "Come to me, Lumina! It's been so long, my dear child. You have returned." Her voice, familiar and unknown, drew me to her.

The warmth and love I felt was that of a long-lost lover. It was that of a mother and child reunited. It was that of love songs and love stories and places good and pure. The love I felt was the love that saves nations and builds temples. Love that makes the flowers bloom and the trees dance. It was love that flowed like water over and through me.

She said, "Come to me," and she called me Lumina.

I dove into the well. Down, down, down…

"Yes… come. Water is the way."

I heard myself say aloud, "Nothing but love." And it flowed over, through, and beyond me.

Down through the water I swam. It was dark like an obsidian chasm, an absolute erasure of light, and as it got even darker, water rushed over my body. I didn't so much as hear the words; I felt them as I was flowing through the water. The barely audible voice whispered to me, "Don't be afraid of the dark." *Woosh* … "You need to travel through the darkness. Shhhhhhh … Not all life is light. Ahhhhhh … come! The dark is necessary. You need not be afraid. Down, down, down. You are still breathing. Yes, breathe in a new way. Come with me! Travel down into my belly through time, through space, through dimensions into the heart of everything, into the heart of my center of my being, into the heart of all things that were, that will be, and are! Let go! Allow yourself to ride, to slide, to go down, down, down. Trust me, my darling."

And even though I knew I didn't speak, I answered, "Yes, yes, I will follow…"

My hair and dress floated behind me. Scenes of memories flitted by me. There I was at six years old in a swimming pool. I saw a brief image of me riding my bike down a hill for the first time. In another, I was joyously leaping into a pile of leaves. But then, as I seemed to accelerate, there was no more time for memories.

There was no time for anything except falling, flowing down. Flashes of light appeared in the dark—spotted lines and swirls—and then the water felt almost viscous. It had a texture at times, and in places, it felt like tunnels lined with moss. Vines and… were those arms reaching toward me, coming up out of the earth and my surroundings to touch me as I flew through the earth? I heard a hum—the hum of the earth like the sound of om, and interspersed, the sounds of screaming passed by me and through me. The churning of water poured through my being, through my head and through my memories, clearing out everything.

Through the Well

As I was flying through the earth, I could see a tiny speck of light way off in the distance. It was like being on a train, going through a deep, dark mountain or underground tunnel. It starts as a speck, but as the train hurdles down the track, that pinpoint begins to get bigger and bigger as it engulfs you and you resurface in the light. The light pulled me in the same way. Physically, I felt like I was going up toward the light. Up, up, and up until I could see the reflection of a little girl staring back at me. Then it was black again.

When I came to, I was looking at the scene through what appeared to be a blurry window. On the other side, I saw an image of a familiar-looking little girl. She had two long, white-blonde pigtails with ribbons pulled up tightly on the top of her head. Her face was small and childlike, but her big green eyes were wise. What on earth was she doing? Why was she just staring? *She's saying something*, I thought. I could see her little lips moving.

"Well, hello there, Spirit of the Well!" proclaimed the little girl.

I could make out what she was saying, even though I couldn't see her clearly. I could read her lips perfectly, but I wasn't sure I understood what she said. I said to myself, confused, "Spirit of the Well? I'm not a spirit." *Where am I?*

I tried to say, "Hello, little girl!"

But she continued, "My name is Wilumina Florida Pearl."

I said aloud, from what seemed to be inside the well, "What? Wait! Is that me? What the fuck? What am I doing?" *God I was a quirky little kid, talking to a well.*

She—or was it me? Okay, *she* went on as if orating a formal and important introduction.

"Most everybody calls me Lu, except my mom. She calls me by my whole name, especially when I'm in trouble. My special name, my secret name, is Lumina. Nobody knows about that name except you and me. Let's keep it that way right now. Okay, Lady in the Well?"

She went on. "People ask me why my middle name is Florida. They say, 'That's a weird middle name!' But I don't mind it too much because of the reasons for it. My mom told me she named me Florida after the best vacation time she'd ever had. So every time she says my name, Wilumina Florida Pearl, it makes her happy. My mom isn't happy much, so I like that my name brings a little smile to her face every now and again. My first name, Wilumina, is such a long name. I like it! My momma and my daddy's families are from the South. I think it's a family name. Like I said, most everybody just calls me Lu. I like that there aren't any other Wiluminas at my school, or ever! I'm the only one! My dad says my name makes me special. Personally, I wish my name was 'Lumina.' Lumina is everything bright, sunny, and sparkly. Everything I wish I could be!" She paused. Her little upper lip twitched a bit as she wrinkled her nose and rubbed her eyes with a tiny, closed fist, struggling to push back some feeling. She steeled herself and smiled big, then said, "I really like my long blonde hair."

Keeping the smile plastered on her face, she puffed up her little chest and explained, "When I run really fast and I jump off the jungle gym, my hair and my dress always fly behind me like wings. Or a cape of a superhero!"

As I listened to her, I thought, *Oh my God! That memory! That's the memory that came to me in the water.*

She continued, "Sometimes when I'm swimming, I let it glide around my face. I go upside down and then quickly, just like a mermaid, I swim backwards. Did you know that only mermaids can change direction so quickly underwater?" She answered herself, "Well, mermaids and a few fish, I suppose. Oh, and seahorses. And of course hummingbirds, but they don't swim, they fly… but you probably already know that! Anyway, I go backwards, and all my hair moves forward until it's in front of me and I can see it. I like when I swim backwards and sideways and it floats in front of me like seaweed."

Yes, I remember this! I was always in the water. Usually by the end of the summer, my hair was bright green from the chlorine. My hair pretty much looked like seaweed under that water. *I must not be more than four years old here.* Then, realizing that I was feeling quite alone, I asked the water, "What am I looking at? What's happening?"

The little girl who was me went on. "When I'm floating or when I'm flying off a ledge, my name is Lumina, Star Seed Child of the Light. I pretend I can fly like a bird!" She pumped her little arms up and down really fast to illustrate what she meant. "I also sometimes pretend I'm a beautiful mermaid. I pretend I'm anything other than what I am." She gave out a little sigh and then asked, "Lady in the Well, can you keep my secret for me? I trust you! Oh wait—my momma is coming!" Then she threw a penny in the well. "I'll be back later!"

And just like that, she was gone.

The penny cascaded down past my face. I reached out to grab it, and nothing was there.

I said, quite aloud, to myself, "Okay—wait now! Cut! Show's over! What's happening?" My heart started pounding, and I felt dizzy. *A little while ago, I was at my mother's funeral, and now I'm supposed to believe I've been sucked underwater or under something to Newport Beach, California? And Newport Beach in 1972? Am I dead? I thought when you died, you went up! I went down! Wait? Am I dead and in hell? I know I did some things wrong and was mean at times, but truly, whoever it is I'm talking to or whoever's controlling this… do you really think I deserve to be in hell? I mean, I cuss a lot, and yeah, I haven't recycled like I should, and okay, okay, I cheated on my boyfriend in college and never told him. But seriously, I thought I'd have to do some really, really bad shit to get sent to hell. What kind of hell is this?*

Then the voice came back again. "Hahaha, Wilumina. Is there really a hell?"

"What? Hello?" I said and shot a glance around. It made the images in front of me ripple. "Who's speaking to me? Why can't I see you?"

"You'll see me soon enough." Her voice was kind and strong. A deep voice, raspy and full of history and wisdom.

The voice continued, "Isn't hell what you make of your life on earth? Do you really think there is a red-horned villain deep underground that's waiting to burn all the bad people? Perhaps hell is a construct that was depicted in early Christianity to keep people in line and to keep them tithing to the church. There is an underworld, but it is nothing like what you're thinking about. The Earth is composed of density and levity. It is water and air. It is shapes and particles. It is spacious and closed off. Hell is something you bring with you. Normally, you would not be visiting us in the middle of your stay on Earth, but you have been called back to us to do some important work—work that is part of your destiny, part of your learning and experience on Earth. You fell through the well, yes. But it wasn't an accident. You were summoned."

"Summoned? By whom?"

"Before we get to that, I want to tell you who I am and what is going on."

"Please!" I said, less of a question and more of a demand.

"I am Kelda. I am one of your guides. It is a great and distinct honor to be in your service."

An image of a woman came into focus. She had raven-black hair and white skin. Her hair was swaying branches of moss and fronds that floated around her. Her skin was almost translucent. I could see through her, yet she seemed solid and real. Her body was there, but I couldn't quite see it clearly. She was dressed in a gown that flowed like water, air, earth, and sky. It was constantly changing. "My guide? I have guides?" I asked.

"Yes, your guide. You have many guides. You have more than most. I am the voice and form of all of them. Know that I am the voice of many but the formation of one. Don't try to focus on all my edges and structure. Just accept that I am here for you. I am an angel assigned to you to help and support you on your mission on earth so your soul can evolve, and you can ascend your spirit to its highest potential.

"I am an arm of God. I mean, I am God just like you are God, but you have grown up separate from that knowledge. Everyone is God. We are all arms or branches of God. Think of it like branches on a tree. In the Tree of Life, we are the branches. We are all part of the same formation, all linked to the main trunk and roots of the tree, but we are the arms of the tree. We are the leaves, the arms, the substance that makes up the Tree of Life. And though we are not the roots, we are still part of the same organism and part of the same creation. That is how we are all connected as God. My Godness is in the other realm, and I have been given the distinct pleasure of watching you grow and evolve your Goddess. Everyone is summoned at some point in their lives to do this work. You've had many lives. With each new life, you have forgotten things. It's time to remember."

In the Well with Kelda

I was still blinking with utter disbelief at what I was experiencing. But there we were, inside a well, looking up at me, my life, my world taking place in 1972.

"You said it's time to remember, Kelda. Time to remember what?"

"It's time for you to shift your life into something different than what has been. There are aspects of your soul."

"How do I do that?"

"It's time to remember what you came to Earth to be. Like mixed-up luggage wrongly claimed at the airport baggage claim. you have been trying to make yourself comfortable with the wrong owners. You have given meaning to your life through the eyes and expectations of others. We are going to help you understand how you got here and how to claim your life back from its wrong owners. Does that make sense at all?"

"I think so. There's this book that I used to read to my children when they were little called *Are You My Mother?* It's about a little bird that hatches out of his egg while his mom is out finding a worm for him. He jumps down from the nest and starts on an adventure trying to locate his mother. He runs into many different characters and asks each of them, 'Are you my mother?' In the end, the giant tractor he calls a snort delivers him back to the nest, just in time to see his mother flying back with a worm. He can identify her because he knows what and who is not her. So yeah, sort of the same thing? Am I right?"

Kelda smiled. "Yes, yes, I suppose you are. You can think of this as Earth plane extra-credit work." She let out a little chuckle and then said, as she reached out her hand, "So hold my hand. Let's dive in, and I'll give you a little lesson on what is happening right now.

"Think again about that beautiful child you just gazed up at through the water. I want you to breathe deeply—in through your mouth and out through your mouth. I want you to start to concentrate on love. Sit back in the water and then lay back. Close your eyes."

"Okay…" I hesitated for a moment, unsure of what actually was and what was not. "I'm not going to drown? You promise? This is so weird!" Slowly, I breathed in. "Okay."

Kelda looked at me and asked, "Are you drowning now as you are talking to me?"

"Point taken." I lay back and relaxed into the water, allowing the rules of earthly experience to drift away. The water engulfed me. I was aware that I was floating in front of Kelda, breathing in and out water in a symbiotic relationship with it. Embryonic, suspended, safe, and held. Was Kelda floating too?

"Let me show you how it's all connected. Let me show you why and how you are here. So, to review, the water from the well, the water from the underworld, is not actually *water*. The underworld isn't literally underground. Even though it feels like it is. Immaterial. Intangible, yet it exists. It's connected to the heavens and the stars, but it's represented as an underworld. And so we travel through the underworld, just like the heavens. It's expansive and light and dark and cloaked in the ethereal.

"You've been taught all your life to be afraid of the mystical, magical realm of nature, like fairies or earth spirits or anything of the earth. Another way that Christianity cut everyone off from the beautiful magic of Mother Earth is that anything associated with the feminine—the womb, dirt, moss, grass, and blood—they were made bad. The magic of the earth was erased from the experience of the mystical and from religious teachings.

"You were told that the only way through to love and safety was through a man. Through a male God. Through a male Jesus. Through men in your life. You were taught that anything feminine was dangerous, evil, and wicked. And you and I know that at this moment we are technically in the underworld. There is nothing wicked about us. Am I right?"

I silently agreed. "But how did I get here? How do I make connections to the under and upper worlds? You're right—I thought angels were only in the heavens. But the way you explain this to me, I kind of get it. Is it that you're both heaven and earth, star and sea, earth and sky?"

"All will be answered," Kelda said. "Come travel with me. Take my hand. By now, I believe you trust me."

I answered, "Yes, I do."

"We will be back in plenty of time. Let's go. Come on.

"Deep breath in, deep breath out. Connect with your inner love. Connect even further down into the crystalline center of the earth, into the womb of the Mother. The great alchemist. Mother Earth, Pacha Momma, Momma Gaia, connect down. Know that anything you need to let go of—anything you fear, anything you are struggling with—she will absorb it. She will transmute it and send it right back to you with love. Can you feel it? Feel the water's flow. Now, connect up through the crown chakra through the light of the stars and through the angels. I'm going to show you how that works.

"Breathe in and breathe out and travel up. Breathe in, breathe out, and travel up through the stars through the hemisphere. Do you see how it became black again? Just like the earth? There is black, there is light, and there are stars, and there is a whole other universe you belong to, my dear. Be showered with light. You are a star seed. You are a light bearer, and this journey is to connect you with your roots, with your body, and with your love of the unity of everything that is. I know it's easy for you to connect to the stars and to spirit and the world of God—the truth that is love but not the truth that is judgment, wrath, or vengeance. Hear the water splashing around you. Trust the water to hold you while you connect with the stars, with your angels, and with your guides.

"Just as I was with you in the water, I am with you in the stars. Let us show you the beautiful magic that we've created, that the angels have created, and let the Mother and Father show you their magical work and their amazing powers. My Sisters and Brothers, the sages and guides, guide you. Take a deep breath! Breath is the way to the heartbeat. Breath is the way to the pulse. So travel with me, and let me show you the beauty of trees.

"Trees are one of our finest symbols of the Universe, of the connectedness of all things. Look into the center of a tree trunk, and all you see are spirals and layers. Trees are the pathways between the under and upper worlds. If you looked down on the planets orbiting the sun, they would create a celestial spiral. If you looked down on the galaxy, it would create a spiral as well … like a tree. There are so many ways to connect. Tree branches reach for the sky, and the tree's roots dig deep down in the earth. Do you remember your special climbing tree? That tree on the corner, in front of Sadie's house? It was special for you because it was truly connected. Can you remember climbing it?"

"Yes, I remember it had little alcoves and divots where I could put my hands and feet. It had a big, sturdy trunk and sturdy branches that came out from there. And then from there were hundreds of smaller but sturdy branches, and from there, thousands of tiny branches that bore hundreds of thousands of leaves. Now that I think about that tree and all trees in a different way, it helps me understand how we are all connected like trees. Every branch, limb, and leaf is important and necessary. No less important than another. I loved that tree! I would climb that tree and swing from the branches. There were lower ones I could swing from, and they would give, so I could get a big swing going. Then I would climb up to the higher branches and hide there. I would read, and I would sing a secret language in songs. It was my own language. I always thought it was silly. My mom would get annoyed by the sounds. But up in the tree, I could sing quietly where she couldn't hear me."

"Do you know that you were aiding many souls in that time? You lit up yourself and the tree with the magic of those words. It was your star seed language, and you were calling the souls to Sadie's house."

"I did not know that! Wow! That's so strange. I used to sing or, like, hum to myself anytime I was in that tree. Sadie was the kind lady who lived on the corner. She was small and slight. She wore cardigans that connected together at the neckline with a brooch that had two chains on either side. She wore simple pressed shirts with elastic-waist pull-on pants or a loose-fitting, straight up and down house dress. But always the cardigan. It was never on her arms, come to think of it. It hung there, magically held by that brooch, making her look as if maybe she was wearing a super-hero cape. She always wore her hair in a bun of what looked like spun white sugar on the top of her head.

"There were always plates of cookies. Not very many, just a few 'so I didn't ruin my supper.' I drank Kool-Aid with her and ate cookies. She served those sandwich cookies, like an Oreo but not. They were lemon or vanilla, and you could pull them apart. They had a little circle on the top where the frosting poked through. She would also have those waffle cookies with layers and layers of crispy, crunchy cookies. They were wafer thins, the little store-bought kind, and they were just delicious! There was a little kid-sized rocking chair and a collection of cloth dolls with yarn hair. They all smelled a little bit like her, and I always had one in one hand and a cookie in the other when I was there."

Kelda nodded her head in agreement and gave me a sweet, knowing smile. "That's a beautiful story about your memories with Ms. Sadie. I know she was a safe and wonderful place for you to find respite from the storms of your life. Sadie's home on Haven Street, however, was so much more than what you remember as a child. While Sadie's home was real to the person living in their day-to-day life, there was a very magical other side to Sadie's house that the normal person could not ever imagine seeing. You never saw it as a child, even though you were a part of it. Most people come through Sadie's in between life transitions. Mostly after they have died and are reckoning with their past life on Earth, deciding where to go next.

"You see, even when a body dies, my dear, the soul goes on. The soul continues to evolve from life to life. You have been called in to make some game-changing adjustments and take in some lessons and heal before you die. Midlife, and here you are. We knew you would be here visiting us earlier than others; we just weren't sure when. So, while the mail carrier delivered the mail and little girls from down the street came over for cookies and to play dolls, Sadie's house had a much greater purpose than what meets the eye. Her house was also a place of respite and a way station for souls. Think of a way station for a train, a place where people stop to eat and rest when they are on a long trip. Not a destination but a stop where people rest and perhaps get information or instruction on the next leg of their soul's journey.

"When you were small, you were connected to the magic but were unaware in your human or earthly being consciousness. Lu, you called the magic in through the trees. The magic swirled into Sadie and Sadie's home, and Spirit asked her to help. Sadie just followed suit and said, 'Okay.' It was no accident that she lived in that little house on the corner for so many years. Even after her children had moved away and her partner had passed, she was, in a way, waiting for you, or someone like you, to come and do exactly what you did. You opened the portal for her and for us. Oh, Lu, it was lovely. Not only did she open space for traveling souls, but she also began healing souls. But we aren't going to go into that too much right now. What is important for you to understand is that the song and the magic and the calling of souls has been with you always."

I said, still confused, "So what you're telling me is that I time traveled in a way, not in my actual body but my ethereal or energetic body, and I am here to help me? Like it's me, my soul, but not me as I know myself to be in my body that I inhabit in the day-to-day world that I know as earth. Is that right, Kelda?"

Kelda replied, "Yes, and your younger you is here to help you in a way as well. It is time to remember … to reconnect. Take my hand, Wilumina."

Kelda looked deep into my eyes and said, "We will take some time with Ms. Sadie in a little while. Right now, Lu needs us to focus on her and help her with her healing and her survival. Close your eyes now, my child, and take a deep breath in and out, just like I showed you before. Travel with me through the well, back to your childhood."

That same sense of energy filled my body. A hum returned to my ears. It wasn't scary this time. I trusted Kelda. I heard in the distance, "Wiluminaaa, Wiluminaaa."

Kelda said, "Repeat after me: nothing but love, nothing but love, nothing but love." I repeated those words, or, rather, we repeated them over and over, and everything went dark.

I heard Kelda say, "Water is the way, my dear; water is the way, water is the way." I heard water swishing and swirling. My body began to expand and contract. I felt that same propulsion forward that I felt when I first dove into the well. I had to let go, trust, and allow my spirit to fly through the water, through the darkness to the light.

"Keep repeating, 'Nothing but love.' Breathe deeply in and out. Hold on to my hand … I won't let go." This time, I had pure love holding my hand.

Newport Beach, the Alley behind Havens Street, 1972

When I opened my eyes, we were standing in the alley behind my old home on Havens Street. We were out of the well. It still felt watery, but now we were floating above this vision in the street, rippling and cascading as we watched.

"Why are we in this alleyway?"

"Watch and listen. You will see."

And there I was! I was coming out of my gate. I loved playing at the playground of the church; it had such a great jungle gym. I can't believe my mom let me go alone! It was such a different time then. I think she was always happy to just get me out of the house and outside. Me too, I suppose!

"Where am I going?"

"Watch."

"Ahh, the juniper cave! I loved that little cave! I would hide there a lot. I guess I was creating my own secret womb. Again in the trees, plants, and bushes, and always in the dirt and mud—climbing in, on, over, and around trees and bushes. Look at that. I am invisible! Wow! Am I okay?"

"Well, you often went under this bush or up in the tree when you needed some time to sort things out or to escape the chaos of your family's emotional world at home. You were a pro at making forts and hiding places and cubbies. They were usually outside in a place to cuddle up and be held."

"I shared that cave with only one other person, Scotty. He was my good friend. He and I played together a lot. We must have often found each other alone outside, as little kids do. It was so easy to make friends. Boy, girl, none of it mattered at that time. I was so unaware of my body and my specialness of being a girl. But I was quickly learning.

"I'll never forget the smell or the feeling I had in that little cave of juniper and cement. I'll never forget how the wet earth and crushed pine needles below mingled with the damp juniper branches and the cement wall of the church. On one side was the church wall, painted gray and covered with stucco. It seemed like every building was covered in sprayed-on cottage cheese back then. Our particular wall or corner of it was bare of its cottage cheese covering, low at the base. It had peeled off from years of water and rain. The cement was exposed and drenched from the earlier rain. It had that particular wet cement smell, like a wet sidewalk after the first summer rain."

We stood there, Kelda and I, transfixed on these two little kids: Scotty and me. They climbed into the cave and disappeared. We went in too. Above and around them were juniper branches smelling dusty and spicy and still dripping a bit from the rain.

The church had been landscaped with low-maintenance juniper bushes and shrubs. Every so often, the gardeners would come through and shape them into mounds and orbs of different shapes and sizes. They created little caves and tunnels under and throughout the shrubbery. It was so much fun to climb through them. They were dark and mossy and rich with dirt and the tangy smell of juniper. The experience of climbing through the juniper caves as a child was much like part of my journey through the underworld.

It was like we were right there with them, but we weren't. We were observing—observing everything and experiencing everything from her (my own) perspective. So, there in the back corner of the church, right by the alley, the bushes opened up just enough to allow two small children to climb inside. The branches made a prickly ceiling just high enough for the two of them to feel hidden from the world. They put their sweatshirts on the ground to cushion their knees from the prickly needles that crunched under them as they shimmied their way in.

Lu had a look in her eyes, excited and warm at the same time. A charge of electricity buzzed between them.

I turned and looked at Kelda, emotion welling up in my eyes. "I remember! Oh God!"

Kelda looked at me calmly and full of love and said, "Yes, that's right; God is here too!"

I went on. "I remember, earlier in the day, we had been climbing and running around on the church playground. I was such a tomboy. But I was also a 'pretty little girl.' I think my mom thought if she dressed me in dresses all the time, I would learn to be more ladylike, less brazen, and sit in the sand and play make-believe tea with all the other pretty little girls. But me? No. I had other interests. I wanted to climb and swing and run with anyone who would join me. It was usually boys who joined me.

"Scotty and I were swinging, spinning, and looping around the jungle gym when my dress flew up, exposing my underwear. They were ripped of course, because most of my panties got torn. It's hard to not tear up your underwear when you're wearing a dress and climbing over and under fences and walls and shimmying up trees all day.

"My mom and dad were always telling me to keep my legs closed and to sit like a lady and to stop touching or itching 'down there.' They would yell at me for tearing my panties or wearing a dress where they were showing. I had a few favorite dresses that I would wear until they were almost shirts, which was about the time my mom would make me stop wearing them. The shorter ones were better for climbing and swinging since they wouldn't get caught as much as my fuller, longer ones. But I knew that there was something magic about my underwear that was supposed to be kept a secret and not seen by other people, especially not by boys. What I didn't understand was that it wasn't the underwear that was magic. What was underneath was magic! That day, though, he only noticed that girls' underwear was different from boys', and he asked about them."

Kelda and I watched as Scotty asked little Lu, "Lu, can I see your underwear in the front?" Innocent enough for sure.

Lu shut her right eye tight and scrunched up one side of her face in contemplation. She said to Scotty, "No, you can't see them because they were a secret and maybe even magic, and I'm not supposed to show them to anyone ever. Especially not boys." And she ran away from him. She had a cardigan around her waist to elongate her dress. The cardigan was an attempt to nurse at least one or two more wears out of her favorite dress before being yelled at for not being ladylike. But that sweatshirt never did a good job hiding her panties while hanging upside down on the jungle gym and sliding down the slides and climbing over the rope ladders, which were her favorite. She'd twist and turn and giggle as she swung this way and that. Scotty wanted to see them closer.

He caught up to her and asked again. "Please? Please can I see them?"

She scrunched her face again and then shrugged her shoulders and said, "Um … okay." I could see her trepidation, knowing that it wasn't okay to show boys her underwear. I knew it well. I watched as she swallowed down, for the first time, her inner voice and ignored that uncomfortable feeling in her belly warning her. Instead of listening to her inner voice, Lu shifted from her own needs toward wanting to please her friend. Plus, they had a hole in the waistband and were pretty dirty from climbing and swinging all day. I could sense a slight essence of shame. But the shame was in the dirty messiness of her. Anything on display should be perfect, and she was definitely not perfect. She looked around and said, "Rules are dumb. Let's go to our cave, and I'll show you."

He was triumphant! And that made Lu happy. Scotty and Lu conspired together to break her "no see 'em rule." They decided to go out into the alley on the other side of the preschool building. Lu whispered and giggled at the same time and made Scotty a deal. "And you can show me your secret magic underwear too!" she said.

"Deal!" said Scotty, maybe a little too loudly as he nodded his head up and down, and they spit in their hand and then shook on it!

All smiles, they snuck into the alley.

As Kelda and I made ourselves comfortable as silent visitors to Scotty and Lu's "little secret," I turned to Kelda, recalling, "Yes! I remember that deal. And I remember that was the first time I received praise and friendship from a boy for going against 'the rules.' It was like an instinct to give in to what he wanted to protect myself from something worse happening."

I turned to Kelda, my eyes filling with tears of what felt like grief, but I wasn't 100 percent sure why. "Kelda, I'm scared for her, for me."

Kelda silently took my hand and turned to watch the children. My eyes followed hers. Biting my lower lip, I reminded myself to breathe slowly and deeply through my nose. We watched and, silently, together, focused on sending them love. Since it had rained that day, Lu laid down her cardigan, and Scotty put down his sweatshirt, and they crawled in the prickly cave that held such great promises of a world undiscovered, shrouded in possibility and curious electricity.

Kelda sensed anxiety emanate from my spirit. "I'm right here with you, my dear. You will be safe now. It's time to remember." So, we watched as the scene unfolded.

Lu asked Scotty, "Do you really think your underwear is magic too?"

He said, "I think so because one time I got a new pair that had Hot Wheels cars on them, and I wanted to just wear them to school with my new shirt, and my mom got mad at me, too, because I didn't want to wear my Toughskins jeans over them."

Lu thought to herself and said, "So yours must be really magic or special, too, if your mom is hiding yours as well."

Scotty just shrugged as if to say, "Who knows?"

He asked her, "Do yours have a flap in the front that you make yourself go pee-pee from?"

"No. I have to pull mine down to go to the bathroom."

"Number two *and* number one?" he asked.

She said, "Yep, both."

"Oh that sucks! I can make pee-pees without having to pull mine down at all," he said, looking mighty proud of himself.

"You can?" Her eyes got really wide. "Wow! How? Show me!"

Sitting in this scene, knowing that they couldn't see me but hoping that there was a small part of Lu that could sense the love we were sending her, I could see the feeling was electric. Innocence at its finest. Two little children about to discover for the first time what it meant in a physical way to be different from each other.

Perhaps Lu wanted to have a sense of being in control, or perhaps she wanted to continue to elicit that huge smile on Scotty's face, but she said, "First mine."

As carefully as she could without getting poked, they found a part in the juniper bush where they could kind of be on their knees. It felt private and secluded. They both looked like they felt safe and hidden from the rest of the world. Truth be told, they weren't that well hidden, but they had filled in the exposed areas with their own imagination of seclusion, and their singular focus was on the magic underwear.

Lu looked both nervous and confident. She pulled up her dress to show Scotty her panties. Scotty looked at her, somewhat unimpressed, and they both decided they were boring and not much to speak of. Scotty's face fell flat as Lu said, "Well, there they are!"

Together, they seemed unsure of why they were such a big deal. "My mom bought me good underwear and then everyday underwear. The good ones I wore to church on Sunday, and they had flowers and ruffles around the edges," she said, hoping to impress him with a promise of something better.

"These ones are my everyday underwear. I just have ones in a few different colors, that's all." They were plain, no ruffles or embellishment save for a small little bow sewn onto the front waistband.

He shrugged again, and his face broke out in a giant smile. "Well, those are lame. Wait till you see mine!"

Kneeling down, he unzipped his Toughskins jeans with the reinforced knees and pulled down his pants all the way to his knees.

"Yours are *way* better!" His underwear had stitching and flaps and panels, and where all of the stitching was, they were different colors.

He said, "These are also just my okay underwear. My Hot Wheels ones are my favorite!"

Scotty proudly displayed his underwear, his hands on his hips, shaking his bottom back and forth, saying, "Mine are better! Mine are better!" They laughed and agreed that his underwear was way better and made a deal to meet again so she could see his Hot Wheels ones.

They sat there for what felt like just a moment, digging in the moist earth and looking at the roly poly bugs that were under the bed of crushed pine needles. They looked above at the branches and fronds of the juniper bush. There were spiderwebs tucked here and there, and they looked with gratitude at them. Scotty looked at Lu and then chuckled a bit and said to the spider weaving a web in the corner, "Thanks for letting us share your space with you."

I looked at Kelda, winked, and said, "If they only knew!"

The spider turned and, what looked to me like appreciation for the acknowledgment, raised its head a bit and got back to work making a new strand of his silky home come to life. From their breath and shared body heat, the little space was warm and comfortable. Scotty never really pulled his pants back up; he just sat on his knees digging around. Plus, I think he was proud of how impressed Lu was with his underwear. It was a quiet and sweet moment shared between the two of them and the security of the juniper cave.

That's when Lu noticed he had a bump in his underwear where the stitched flap was. Her little face ever so slightly squinched up on the right side. In between looking at spiders and bugs, she would look at that lump. I could see her little brain working out the possibilities for that little bump. She never did or said anything. But I knew that this exchange of wonders and interests in each other's bodies wasn't over. I knew she wanted to know more about it.

They lost track of time.

Before they knew it, it was late. We heard Scotty's brother, Todd, calling him for dinner. Scotty's brother was older, maybe thirteen or fourteen at the most. But to them, he was way older. He was often in charge of Scotty and was pretty bossy if not downright mean to him. Lu didn't like Scotty's brother.

I couldn't remember exactly why she didn't like him, but I clearly knew she just didn't. A current of fear and rage swept through my spirit. I didn't mention it to Kelda, but I could tell she knew I was feeling something.

Scotty's eyes lit up at hearing his brother calling. He thought his brother was everything and jumped to attention when he heard him call. He pulled his pants back up. Scrambling, he buttoned the top button of his pants, and they climbed out of their secret, magical hiding spot just as Todd was coming down the alleyway. They had pine needles and spiderwebs in their hair and mud on their knees and clothes. Struck by the change in temperature,

Lu gave a little shiver, reached in the branches, and grabbed her sweatshirt. She and Scotty didn't think anything of it.

But Todd looked at the two of them standing there. Both kids felt a little bit guilty for having a secret and breaking rules, but neither was sure why. The side of Todd's mouth curled up, and his eyes narrowed as he eyed the scene—pine needles, soot, and all. Then Todd said something to Scotty that Lu felt was the strangest of all: "That's my little brother! Already a lady's man!" Todd winked at them, smiled, and nodded his head up and down a few times.

Scotty smiled big, puffed up his chest, and said, "Yeah," feeling so proud of himself. Lu looked confused. Her eyes darted back and forth between the two of their faces, trying to understand. Scotty didn't know what Todd was talking about either. Then Todd clipped Scotty on the back of the head and told him to zip up his fly.

Scotty quickly zipped up his fly and then looked at Lu with a "Whoops, what's a kid to do" kind of shrug in his shoulders. Todd's eyes lingered on Lu for a moment too long. He stared at her in that funny way, half grinning and half scowling. It was a look that made Lu shrink and look at the ground.

Unaware of her movements, she gripped her tummy with both arms. But then Todd was smiling, which confused her. He seemed happy that he was making her so uncomfortable.

That's when I looked at Kelda and said, "I hate that kid!"

Kelda said, "We don't hate here. But you are allowed the feeling associated with hate. This boy is in a lot of pain. You are feeling his collective pain and the pain of Scotty's family."

I was feeling my own damn pain too! I replied to Kelda, "I didn't know then what I was feeling, let alone the ability to name it or even understand why it felt so confusing. Now, as a grown woman, I know. It was the look of a perpetrator!"

Kelda again just silently looked back at the scene unfolding. I followed her gaze and looked back at Scotty. He was shuffling his feet in a dance of awkwardness. His face had turned red, but he was smiling at Lu too.

Lu seemed to shrug off the discomfort and wiped it from her face. I could see that she began to question her inner knowing that something was off. This was a moment when Lu's internal safety compass was telling her something wasn't right. But just as she felt the twinge of warning, it seemed to disappear just as quickly.

Was she just making things up in her mind about the meaning of the look from his brother?

My hand touched my face as I looked again at Kelda. *Ugh! No!* "Why do we do that? Why did I do that?"

Kelda looked at me and said, "You do that for many reasons. In your life, because it wasn't safe in your home to voice your feelings, you learned not to trust yourself. You learned to question your own inner wisdom because you didn't have a safe adult to help show you the way. That's what happens to kids when they aren't taught how to trust themselves. They feel things and then get a different signal from their parents, so the message from inside is silenced. Your home was not safe, and that caused your inner voice to be silenced as well."

This felt stunning and true.

We watched as Scotty and Todd waved goodbye and Lu ran to the alley gate that made up the anterior wall of her backyard. She went through the gate. We followed closely behind. With a heavy sigh and a shudder, I could see Lu was releasing more of the "bad feelings" inside. She was less conflicted than before and seemed determined to shrug away the yuckiness inside.

Walking directly to the wishing well, she stopped and made a wish "Dear wishing well, I would like to be able to go back to mine and Scotty's juniper cave again soon, even though I don't like his dumb brother." And then she went to her house to clean up for dinner.

I turned to Kelda. I was confused and felt a welling inside that was calling me to understand why she would want to go back after what just happened.

Kelda replied, "Tell me about that feeling you got when Todd looked at you."

Reflecting, I began to explore what the feeling was. I knew on that day the feeling started to have a life of its own, as if it were alive inside of me. The feeling lived in my belly. Describing it to her, the feeling was a mix of emotions. "It was scary, admired, and dirty all at once. It was confusing and comforting all at the same time. I have experienced it many times. It always started with a look a perpetrator gave me. From that night on, the feeling was with me. Always below the surface, needing to be managed so it didn't overtake me. It lived snuggly inside of me and felt familiar, like an old friend. Only it wasn't out for my own good. The feeling had its own agenda that I could never fully trust, only learn to manage. Metaphorically, it reminds me of what it feels like to be a kid sitting in front of a warm fire, with a blanket, a long stick, and plenty of marshmallows to roast. Except the feeling didn't know discernment or when it had enough. It only knew that it was to fill my insides and keep those places inside of me from knowing what had happened. Its purpose was to distract me, but it was drawn to people who were inherently unsafe.

"The feeling itself is hot and sticky, sweet and tempting. Like the marshmallow, one was never enough. I would tell myself I could always eat one more. One more—that's all I would need. The desire to consume the marshmallows would grow inside me, and I craved more without remembering that too much would make me sick.

"The thing is marshmallows are like compliments and other things you crave but that hurt when they go too far. Compliments from just about anyone were like a two-sided sword; my inner self wanted them so badly, but the part of me that knew the truth would push them away. How could I be good and so bad at the same time?

"And yet it was always tempting in the same way it is to eat just one more marshmallow.

"*Maybe this time it won't make me sick.*

"The desire to get closer and closer to the thing that tempted me, regardless of the danger, is always present. Even to this day, that push and pull lives within me.

"That day with Todd was like a compliment from a stranger. On the surface, the look he gave me would have made anyone excited. Made them feel wanted and important. I wanted that too. But it also made me feel like I was being drawn into the fire. Drawn to the place where instead of eating one marshmallow, they were involuntarily being shoved down my throat. No matter how I tried to stop, they just kept coming, making me sicker and sicker. Yet on the surface, it was just a harmless marshmallow. A fluffy, white, sugary treat that made kids smile in their toes when they got a chance to eat one.

"Even at four years old, I knew there was something wrong with the look Todd gave me. I couldn't put it into words of course, and what I'm saying now is from an adult, but I knew then something was wrong. His look was both tempting and terrifying and made me feel gross inside. I remember that night I went to bed without dinner because this sick feeling came over me, and I couldn't eat anything. And of course, I could never explain to anyone what it meant. As I got older, and men would look at me like he did, I would have that same sticky, sweet feeling followed by terror. No one would understand why a compliment from a man would send me into this whirlwind of emotions. So, I would swallow all of it. The feelings, the fear, just so I would look normal because no one understood or knew.

"It became normal to live this way, and I disconnected from all the signs my body gave me when the marshmallow feeling came up. And then, *as if I needed more*, somehow, whatever happened, it became my fault.

"If a man looked at me with lust or longing, I somehow invoked that look in his eyes.

"If a man got mad at me or raged at me, somehow that was my fault too.

"I brought out these experiences in other people. It was me. I was the odd one. I was not normal. And because I couldn't, or didn't, trust my feelings when a boy looked at me like Todd did, it was my fault whatever came next, because to everyone else, that look was as sweet as a little, innocent marshmallow.

"As an adult, I can see more of the separation now. I know when people look at me, they are having their own experience, and it's not because of me or even about me. I get the same sick feelings, but I know how to manage them and keep myself safe. But I wasn't empowered. I wasn't taught to speak up. I wasn't taught to be bold. I wasn't taught to object or to protest. I was taught to eat people's opinions, whether they were good or bad. I took them in like a hungry little girl waiting for her marshmallow, never knowing if it would be a landslide of perversion or an innocent, sweet treat.

"Does that make sense, Kelda?"

"Yes, my dear. Yes it does."

"Kelda, this memory, this was the first night it happened, right? This thing with Todd was the source of all the sticky marshmallows shoved at me without my consent. Wasn't it?"

Kelda held my hands as a single tear fell from her eye. She gently nodded her head, looked at me, and said, "Water is the way, my dear. Water is the way. Follow the tears toward love. In the end, Lu, all we have is love."

We repeated together, "Nothing but love, nothing but love, nothing but love..." as we followed that tear back to the well.

Once it felt like we had settled, and we had gone through the experience of moving through time and space, I needed a minute to understand this *love* and just be in it.

I asked Kelda, "Can we take a moment? Can I do that?"

Coming back into the well, I was able to understand more clearly that the well was a portal of some sort, a place where the veil between what was linear and what was unexplainable collided. It was a space between time and place. Neither here nor there. A space where I could be with Kelda and catch my breath and float in the warm, energetic waters like a womb. It was like we were under water but not wet. I floated away to a space of ultimate love and comfort.

"You don't need to ask permission to rest, Lu; just let me know, and we will rest. I am not in charge of you. I am a guide for you."

So I rested for bit, but then she alerted me that Lu still needed our help, and we weren't done with our time with her in this experience. We would have time to rest and talk later, once we arrived at Sadie's house. Lu needed us, and it was time to return to her.

Kelda looked in my eyes, and a tiny tear fell as she said, "Water, my love, is the way… water is the way."

And then, as if I knew exactly what to do and say, I turned to her and said, "Nothing but love, nothing but love, nothing but love."

And with those words, we became ready to go back to little Lu. We closed our eyes and swirled through time and space, flowing in from the dark to the light, and then we just walked in through the back wall of little Lu's childhood home.

"Why not the door?"

Kelda looked at me, threw her head back, and said, "Oops, you caught me showing off!" And there we were in Lu's dining room.

Lu's mom was there.

Wait, stop! I mean, she was my mom!

I exclaimed, "Mom! Mom! Oh my God, Mom, I miss you so much!"

Kelda said sweetly, "She can't hear you, dear. Especially not your mom. She has closed herself from us. She has forbidden any help. Your mom has chosen to do this life on her own. It's a hard path for her but one she will learn great and amazing lessons from to pass into her next life."

"Can I touch her?" I asked.

Kelda's face twitched a bit, and she said, "Typically, we aren't allowed to touch people in the earth plane, but I know how much you love breaking rules, and what are rules if not to bend just a little bit. Go ahead. She will feel your touch as a breeze on her skin and a slight cooling in her system."

There I was, face-to-face with my mother. My beautiful, complicated, loving, and wicked mother. I reached out and touched her face with my hand, and she turned ever so slightly toward my light touch. We were standing there—tuna casserole in her hands and my hands on her face. I breathed in her perfume. *Ahh, Charlie.* She always wore the perfume called Charlie! She had on a dress. It was a shift to her knees. She was so small and slight. No taller than five foot four and quite slim. She was an absolute picture of beauty. Her hair was longer then, and she had it in two low ponytails at her neck. They draped over her shoulders, and she leaned down to serve the casserole. Even though Kelda said she couldn't tell and wasn't in touch, I swear she knew I was there, and I was openly and freely able to love her for one moment. I loved... I love that woman with a ferocity never equaled by any other love in my life, short of my own beautiful children.

Kelda put her hand on my hands and said, "Remember, we are here for Lu today. You are allowing yourself to be sucked back into your family patterns. Now is not the time to heal the old patterns of wanting to help your mom. That will come later. She has her own journey. We are here for Lu."

"Okay, okay," I whispered. "I love you, Mom. I forgive you, Mom. Please, one day, I hope you are able to forgive me. Thank you for all you have done to grow and heal. Thank you for my life!"

With her hand on my shoulder, Kelda nudged me ever so slightly toward little Lu sitting at the table. "I can assure you she will and has already forgiven you. But at this moment, my dear, we are here for Lu." I turned to the scene unfolding at the dining room table. It was a familiar scene, one I would replay over and over again in my lifetime.

Julia, Lu's mother, asked why Lu wasn't touching her food, and she just said, "I'm not feeling well." Julia sighed heavily and scraped the uneaten tuna casserole back into the pan to be reheated for lunch or dinner another day. Lu didn't like tuna casserole anyhow, so even on a good day, it was a struggle to eat. She usually tried to get away with just eating the crumpled potato chips on top.

I heard Lu say under her breath, "I mean seriously, canned tuna, cream of chicken soup, big, floppy, soggy egg noodles with water chestnuts and peas, all baked together with potato chips on top? So disgusting."

"Yes, Kelda! I don't remember this meal exactly—how could I? But I remember this whole scenario being played out in our household many times. I'm confused why I remember some things very well and why I can't remember other things about my childhood."

Kelda turned to me and said, "Tell me, my dear, what you do remember."

"I knew my mom was angry at me for wasting food. My dad worked for the church across the alley from our little house, and my mom was a part-time nurse. My brother and I were really close in age, and my sister was only three years older. My sister tried to help out as a 'mommy's helper,' but she was only seven, so she wasn't that much help. My mom was often tired and worn out. My dad worked a lot and had a perpetual evening meeting. He was often not home for dinner. Even though he worked a lot, he didn't make much money. He and Mom fought about money a lot. He said because he was doing God's work, he shouldn't make a lot of money. To Dad, money was the opposite of receiving God's love, and, in fact, it blocked one from that love. God was like my dad's own private financial blocker. To my father, accepting the bare minimum and making do were some of his favorite virtues of being a Christian. The desire for anything more was at the worst a sin and at its best unvirtuous.

"We were all to understand this, most importantly Mom, who should have been able to understand and pick up the burden of raising the kids so he could work seven days a week for God. She also had to understand that she needed to earn income to supplement his important work so she could pay for her 'frivolous' needs like her frosty mauve lipstick, the occasional trip to the cinema, and babysitters. She tried but was often reminded of her inability to rise up and support my father's work when we acted up or when she felt shame for her simple dresses and home-set curls. For some reason, she thought that her children's inability to be perfect reflected on her ability to be a good preacher's wife and, therefore, a good and valuable person. But since we were kids and she had unreasonable expectations of us and of herself, she was often tired and distraught and angry at us and herself for not measuring up to her impossible view of what a perfect Christian family looked like.

"I would later learn how to eat through the bad feelings. As a child, I hated it when she would cry because she was lonely and poor and overwhelmed by the trouble the three of us 'caused' her. In actuality, we were just being children, and she was a normal woman with needs and wants that weren't frivolous or shameful. Even at that young age, I had an understanding that Mom's pain and suffering were my fault, and I needed to do as much as I could to protect her from it—thus creating the seed for my own impossible view of what my role would be in my family and then, subsequently, in my own life going forward."

I shook my head and said, "Damn, this was the beginning for me on how to learn to live with feelings that burned hot and sticky and fierce and to smile through the pain, wasn't it?"

"Yes, my dear," Kelda replied. "This is when you began to learn your role as a pain eater in your family. This is when you learned that perhaps it is not safe to share your feelings with your family. Do you recall just a minute ago with your mother? How you wanted to go and help her?"

"Yes."

"And I made you focus on Lu?"

"Yes. That was annoying at first. I felt like you were trying to take me from my mom."

"The truth is what I was actually doing was pulling you out of the cycle of relating solely to your mother's dominating feelings and encouraging you to focus on Lu and taking care of yourself. You have done such a good job caring for others. But you sure haven't done well caring for yourself."

"I can't disagree."

"Can you see how you started to learn?"

"Yes. Loud and clear."

I closed my eyes and began to settle into my soul. I could hear the waves deep within begin to undulate with the rhythm of my breath. I leaned back into the sounds and into the feeling of being held and carried away through water. Kelda's voice rose over this experience, and I heard her say, "My love, water is the way."

On cue, I began to repeat, "Nothing but love, nothing but love, nothing but love."

I began to become one with the flow. With each exhale, I began to allow the pain in the pit of my stomach to rise. Kelda's hand gave me strength to lean into my own healing.

Sadie's House, Somewhere between Here and There, between Time and Space...

And with that, we were back in what appeared to be my neighbor's home but wasn't. It was more ethereal. My head was spinning. "Where are we now? Why are we at Sadie's house? Why does it look kind of different than what I remembered? Who are all these people?"

We were in the living room. The room wasn't full, but there were quite a few people, some sitting together in discussion at the dining table, and others were on the couch. The walls were pink, and even though they were walls, they seemed billowy and translucent. There seemed to be a person in charge of what was going on, but I couldn't be sure. Was she Ms. Sadie from down the street?

Kelda smiled and placed a kiss on the cheek of the person in charge. "This is a place for spirits and guides like me and travelers like you to come and rest and be while they sort out their next move, or before their person calls for them again. Lu is going to need us shortly. Please feel free to ask for a cup of coffee and have a snack. It won't be long. I don't want you to be hungry or tired. You might even want to take a nap. Over there is a wonderful sleep chamber. Just a few minutes in there will rejuvenate your entire body, spirit, and mind."

I decided to go to the sleep chamber and take a little nap. I woke up from my nap rejuvenated and full of energy and love for all the people around me. I suddenly felt as one with them. When I looked around, many of them made gentle eye contact with me, as if to say, "Welcome." Over against a distant wall were several doors where people were standing around as if waiting to go in. After a period of time, I asked Kelda if I could go and see what they were waiting for.

Kelda said, "Of course, my dear. If you feel called to a room, then you must go. Perhaps it is what you need in order to assist Lumina when we go back to her."

I began feeling agitated, even though minutes before I felt a part of something very special. I said, "Hmm, that's cryptic, but okay." My mood continued souring. I was getting restless just sitting, not speaking, and serenely smiling at the other people. I said under my breath, "If I have to smile gently at someone one more time, I might have to turn a table over. Don't these people get sick of being so serene all of the time?"

Kelda, aware of my agitation yet completely unbothered by it, said to me, "Use your agitation and your restlessness to assist you in the room. What you are feeling right now is connected to that room. Don't fight it. Let it assist you in expressing your feelings."

So, I got up and went over to the room. I didn't wait long, so that was good. When I opened the door and walked in, it was dark. I started to feel scared. I was worried that someone was going to jump out and hurt me. This was a familiar feeling for me. I never really knew why. I'd always worried as I jogged at night or went hiking alone that someone would jump out and grab me and hurt me. It had to be some kind of memory of which I was unaware. Anyhow, here I was standing in a dark room. When I looked up, I could see a figure in the distance looking back at me. When I shook my hand, she shook her hand. When I jumped up and down, she jumped up and down. My reflection? Was that crazy-looking person me? Hmmm. She was dressed head to toe in brown burlap. Many, many layers of brown burlap and cloth were hanging off of her all over. It was shredded and hanging down and swayed in a somewhat beautiful way as she stomped and jumped. She had wild white hair that seemed to move with her as she swayed and danced, and on her head was a headdress that was brown as well. The headdress was covered in shells and bones, and there were stones tied to it and dangling from it. They danced and mingled with her wild white hair. The shells made sounds as she jumped and stomped. She held a rattle of shells and seeds in her right hand. In her left hand, she had a basket full of bones. She was shaking that, too, and looking into it, singing and blowing her song into it. She had either dirt or paint on her face, and she looked fierce. She was young but looked old. She was glorious and ugly all at once. She started jumping up and down and yelling, "Hey yaa hey yaaa. Icheeeeayahhhhh!" I realized that, as I stood there watching, I wasn't actually watching but jumping and shaking an invisible rattle in my hand with her.

I started to follow her. Then my movements and her movements became one, and I started to feel the rage and purpose of her dance and chant while jumping, yelping, and screaming. It wasn't necessarily an angry dance, but it was full of purpose, and a sense of rage seemed to guide my steps. It was a dance of war and celebration. Was that possible? We jumped in unison. I could hear drumming in the distance that kept the beat with our dancing and jumping and shouting. It was incredible! The drumming was getting louder and louder.

Around me, a circle of women started forming. There was a line of women coming into focus and circling around me—that was where the drumming was coming from. Each woman had a different skin shade. They made a rainbow of colors from very dark to very pale. Their hair was also a rainbow of beautiful colors: black, brown, red, golden, and white as snow. They were all made up from one another. They were different and the same. Crying and laughing, some screaming and some humming a deep, deep resonant sound, they danced together to the beat of their own drums.

Some of the women held sticks and banged their drums. Others drummed the drums with their hands. They formed a circle. Some of the women sat in the circle on a three-legged stool, stomping their bare feet on the earth; on their feet were rattles similar to what the woman in front of me held in her hands. They all stomped, and while they were fierce and strong, they all looked at me with knowledge and a sense of encouragement for me to let go of my apprehension and just go with the music. Though they said not a word to me that I cognitively understood, I knew they were all there for me. They were my ancestors and my guides coming to show me my power.

I stomped and shouted, "Waaaayyy ooooh wahhhh waaay oooh wahhh!" Then a new sound joined the circle. It was that of howling dogs. Seated between every few women was a big wolf and her small pups on each side of her. They, as if on cue, would howl and bark to the singing and the drumbeat. I was now swaying and stomping in unison with the woman in front of me, arms raised and my face toward the dark night, tears streaming down my face, whirling in circles. The room started to fill with water on the floor from the tears of the women and dogs. As we stomped, the water splashed and splattered all around us, catching some distant light and making a glowing wash of drops and splashes all around us. I was breathing hard but did not feel fatigued.

For a moment, I tried to understand what race or culture they were from, until I realized it didn't matter—we were all part of the same tribe of Mother Earth. We were one. We were expressing rage and power. We were expressing love. We were howling with the mother wolves, the animal guardians that were there to guide us into our sacred, earthy, powerful feminine. This was an expression of the divine feminine that I had never experienced. They all began to stand around me, stomping, crying, and chanting an eerily familiar sound, circling me as I whirled and stomped and screamed. I lost consciousness at one point, even though I kept standing. Their chanting lifted me up, up, up. They continued to stand and stomp around me, the circle getting smaller and smaller until each of them were touching my body. I could feel the panting breath of the dogs around me. They were circling me and lifting me. Coming in from the distance was that same screaming sound I had heard at the well. It surrounded and drowned out everything else: *EeeeeeYaaaaeeeeyaaaayayayayaya!* There were flashes of light like lightning strikes, and then, just like that, the lights went on. I was lying on a dry, clean floor in an empty room; all I could see on the far wall was a neon exit sign flashing on and off. I was wet with perspiration and still breathing hard, but instead of feeling spent, I felt energized. I was alone in the room. I lay there for a moment on my back, looking up at the pink ceiling, smiling and amazed.

"*Damn* that was incredible! Thank you, thank you, thank you!" I got up, and slowly but surely, I walked out of the room.

I walked back into the common room and sat down next to Kelda. She looked at me with a giant smile and simply said, "Hello, dear."

"Hello." I smiled back and let out a big exhale. My entire body was restored and felt powerful.

Kelda looked up at a line of lights along the wall. "Do you see that one there? The third from the middle? That light is for us. When it lights up, we will know it is Lumina. It will be time to go down and be there with her; she will need our support."

"Are you going to explain what just happened to me?"

"All I can say is this: you are going to need to draw on the power of that sacred dance as we go to assist Lu. Remember where you have come from, my dear. Remember that you are loved, you are supported, and you are guided by forces far greater than you could ever muster on your own."

I thought about it for a few seconds, smiled, and replied, "There's no way I'll ever forget." I took a deep breath in and out, and together we sat in silence until the third light from the middle lit up.

Kelda took a deep breath and said, "Follow me, dear." She took a few steps to a landing of sorts and looked at me as a small tear fell from my eye.

As we held hands, she said, "Water is the way, my love. Water is the way."

I replied, closing my eyes, "Nothing but love, nothing but love, nothing but love," and we were back on the playground of the church.

Two Weeks Later on the Playground of the Church in Newport Beach, 1972

Scotty and Lu were playing as they usually did. Scotty was smaller than Lu. He had a face full of freckles and a big cowlick at the front of his forehead that made his hair stand up like a cockscomb. He had bright blue eyes and a sweet disposition. He definitely was too sensitive to belong in his family. I knew that his mom and dad fought a lot and that his dad hit his mom and him on occasion. I had sometimes seen marks on the back of his thighs. He'd say something like, "Oh, I got a whooping last night."

In response to my horror, he'd say it was okay because he deserved it for misbehaving. My parents never hit me. And what child *ever* deserved to be hit? I mean seriously! But to be honest, sometimes I wished I would just get a whooping and not have to endure all of the yelling. Scotty and I were drawn to each other by our mutual understanding that we were a little too sensitive for this tough world we lived in.

So, there on the playground, Kelda and I observed the two of them leaping and climbing over the jungle gym. Scotty's face lit up as if he had just thought about the most wonderful thing ever! He looked at Lu with a mischievous smile and said, "Hey, Lu! Let's go to our cave!"

They hadn't been back since Todd found them a few weeks before. She had been there alone plenty of times. She went there to watch the roly polys and to talk to the spiders. There was a new spider that had made its home in the corner, and she wanted to share it with Scotty. So, her eyes lit up, too, and a big smile broke out across her face at the news that he wanted to go back. "Heck yeah!" They snuck out to behind the church next to the alley, in the corner under the juniper bush, and crawled in. It was just as she had left it: the imprints of one little animal snuggling in the leaves and under the shelter of cover and refuge.

As they crawled in, they both seemed to like it there. Lu looked behind her as she was wiggling her way over, making sure to make enough space for Scotty. "Do you think it's weird that I like little, tiny spaces? I always have. I always make them and find them. It's fun to be hugged by plants and blankets."

As I heard Lu explaining this to Scotty, I turned to the side and said to Kelda, "I believe it was my deep need for safety that drove me to create forts and caves and tiny, safe spaces." Kelda gave my hand a squeeze and remained silent. We watched as these two little children intersected in a way to create a little extra safety in their worlds. They felt invisible there. Safe and protected.

As she got situated, Lu pricked her hand on a dried juniper branch broken off during the latest storm. Or maybe she broke it off at some point while coming and going. She yelled, "Ouch!" and raised her hand to find a thorn from the branch sticking out of it. It had punctured the palm of her hand and was stuck there.

Scotty grabbed her hand and said, "Woah! Dang! That must hurt, Lu!"

Lu said, "It doesn't hurt that bad, but still it hurts!" She shook her hand, but the thorn wouldn't fall off on its own. They laughed at how it stuck in her hand.

Scotty said, "Hold still. I'll pull it out."

She said, "No! Like, no!" Lu's lower jaw jut out, and she was grinding her teeth at the thought of pulling it out. "Ouch. It'll hurt!"

He said, "No, I'll do it quick. Just hold still."

So, she held still, and, trustingly, she lifted her hand up to him. He held it in his, and very gently and quickly, he pulled the thorn from her hand. A bead of bright red blood sprouted from the tiny hole where he pulled it out.

He took his shirt, pushed on it, and said, "Suck on it, and it'll be okay."

So, she sucked on her hand over and over again until. When she stopped sucking and looked at her palm, a tiny drop would form, and she would raise her hand to her mouth once again and lick it off.

Lu paused for a moment and said to Scotty, "Blood tastes strange, doesn't it? Tangy and metal and sweet, like a shiny penny."

She licked the blood off, pressed on it again, held her hand up to him, and asked, "Want to taste my blood?"

He took her hand in both of his hands and slowly pressed it to his mouth. He stuck his tongue out and licked the blood.

They both had a look that came over them, as if they were wondering if it was okay or not.

Lu said, "Do you think you're gonna turn into a vampire?"

Scotty said, "Do you think I could get sick?" They waited a bit, and when nothing happened to him, they both seemed to exhale a bit with relief.

"Kelda, this was such a sweet moment. Thank you for sharing it with me! I remember this vaguely. I remember it made me feel loads of weird things inside for Scotty."

And right after I said that, we watched as Lu, accustomed to pushing feelings aside, pulled her hand away, blushed, and went on with playing with Scotty's Hot Wheels he had brought to share.

We could see Lu getting the quizzical look on her face again. "Can I see your underwear again? I want to know about that bump in your underwear."

"What bump?" Scotty asked.

Lu said, pulling her dress up again, "Well, see, I have the same boring underwear, and I don't have a bump under mine. See? It's smooth here." She rubbed the front of her panties.

He said, "No way!" Then he thought about it and said, "Only if I can see what's inside your underwear first."

Lu said, "Not a chance! *You* show me yours first!"

So, hesitantly, he once again unzipped his Toughskins jeans and pulled them down to his knees. Then she said, "Pull down your underwear." And he did. When he did that, he released his penis from its snug home under the fancy stitching and reinforced jeans. There it was. It was like her little brother's (they had taken baths together), but because it was Scotty's, it felt different to see it. It stood up by itself and looked like a tall mushroom.

She said, "I think that's amazing! Wow!" She wanted to see it and touch it and look at it. She reached out and touched it, and it got a little taller.

"Wow! How weird! How cool!"

Scotty seemed kind of proud too.

As we observed this intimate exchange of innocence and wonder, I realized what a strong voice I had. I turned to Kelda and said, "Wow, where did I get that strong of a voice? And where did it go?"

She said that I had at that age a very strong sense of will and had no problem asking for what I wanted. I hadn't learned to silence my needs so well just yet.

Back in the juniper cave, suddenly above them, a voice boomed, "*Scott?* Scott. Scotty!" It was Todd.

He reached in the cave, pulled Scotty out, smacked him hard, and yanked and marched him home. He said nothing to Lu. She was left there, having gone from feeling exhilarated about her discovery about Scotty to feeling sad and shameful and confused. She sat down on the earth and looked at the ground. Her face scrunched up, and her lower lip started to shake. She started to cry. Lu huddled in her little cave, crying and not really knowing why. After a spell, she crawled out, brushed herself off, and went home. No dinner again that night either. Her soul was munching on roasted marshmallows by the fireside.

They never went back to the cave after that. In fact, she never really played with Scotty again. What Lu didn't know was that he had been beaten by his older brother for letting a girl tell him what to do. Girls weren't supposed to look at his "you know what." He was only supposed to look at girls' things, not the other way around.

Panic suddenly gripped me. "Kelda, how do I know that? Kelda? Who told me that?"

Kelda replied, "Todd. Todd told you, dear. Take a deep breath in and out. Take my hand."

The Bluebird

We arrived a week or so later in Lu's world; she was walking down the alley, coming home from her friend Carla's house.

That's right—Carla! She was my good friend! Carla lived at the end of the cul-de-sac, and I was allowed to walk down there on my own, but only through the alley. My mom wouldn't let me cross streets alone. I was so little. The alley was safer, she said. If only I could have been hit by a car. If only I had known that the alley was the most dangerous place I could be, with Todd looking out for me to "teach me a lesson."

"Why did I just think that? What does that mean? Todd taught me a lesson?" Kelda held my hand and looked down the alley. I thought I might faint. I became weak in the knees. A buzzing was coming over me along with a sense to run away fast.

It was later in the afternoon. The light was that yellow pinkish color, and the shadows were long. It made for a certain darkness in the east corners of the lots going down the alley. Todd and two of his friends came up behind Lu and grabbed her. Todd was thirteen or fourteen. He had blue eyes like Scotty's, but unlike Scotty, his eyes were hard and cold, as if they had already seen a lot of violence at his young age. Todd was the oldest of the three boys. He had ginger-colored hair and a scar over his right cheek that Scotty said was from him trying to protect his mother from his dad's beatings.

He had on a ball cap, so it was hard to see his eyes. But Lu would be able to see that they were dead. Todd was wearing cutoff jeans and an OP tank top. The other two boys must have lived in the neighborhood. One was chubby and smelled like stale Fritos and nacho cheese. His chubby belly hanging out over his too-small tank top bounced as he ran down the alley after Todd, who was pulling Lu back behind the woodpile in the alley. The fat boy had a little bit of hair growing in his armpits, which were dripping sweat as he bounced down the alleyway.

The other boy was thin as a rail and had almost white, long hair that he put behind his ears. The little skinny one had on a green T-shirt that said "I'm a Pepper" with a bottle of Dr. Pepper on the front. His lips and his nose were sunburned, and his hair fell over his eyes. They pulled her into an open part of the alley where the fence separated the house from the alley. There was a spot there that was set back farther than all the others. In that space was a bush with wide leaves on it. Garbage cans and a wood pile provided secrecy. They pulled her into that space, jostled her, and yelled at her.

Lu was tiny and no match whatsoever for three teen boys. It was terrifying to watch; I covered my eyes and kept saying, "No, no, no, no, no."

Kelda looked at me with tears in her eyes too, and said, "This is what happened. This is what you don't remember. I am right here with you. Take my hand. We are going to get through this together."

"Listen, you bossy little bitch!" Todd's words were spitting into her face. "You are not allowed to touch my little brother's dick without letting him touch yours first. I heard you, you bossy fuck. I heard you tell him no. Girls are not allowed to say no to men."

Todd seemed pleased with himself. The two other boys were behind him, saying, "Yeah, bitch! Yeah! No way!"

Todd, feeling bolstered, continued. "You bitches are here to take orders from us and do what we tell you to do!" Todd was full of rage. The scar on his left cheek that usually showed white had turned bright pink as he was yelling at Lu. His cheeks and his neck were flush, and the vein on his neck was pulsing as he threatened her. Lu was struggling to turn her face away and would shut her eyes every now and then to try to avoid Todd's spit that was flying all over her as he whisper-screamed at her.

"We are going to teach you a lesson, you little slut, for doing that to my little brother. Help me, guys!" The two other boys came around Todd's shoulders and took Lu's arms and, kneeling on her shoulders, pinned her down while Todd ripped off her panties. She started to make noise, shouting for help. She started to kick her legs and turn her head, but she was much too small and no match for these boys. To silence her, they lifted her dress up all the way over her head, so it was over her face, and they each took turns poking and pinching her. She was kicking and strug-gling, so the skinny one put his knee on her shoulder to keep her pinned down better.

They stuck their fingers in her and spit on her and made fun of her. "Let me kiss her! I'm feeling horny! Hahaha!" A set of dry, scratchy, cracked lips scraped across her face through her dress, which was twisted up over her head. She could barely breathe.

They smashed themselves on her. One pressed on her shoulders to hold her down while the other pressed on her bottom and legs.

Lu was silent and slowly stopped moving. "Boys do to girls. Girls do not touch boys! Yeah, unless we order you to touch us, then you sure as fuck better!" She had stopped fighting. Her little body lay there motionless.

"Kelda! Did they kill her? Kelda! This is the most horrible thing I've ever seen! Kelda! Help her!"

Kelda directed energy at Lu's motionless body, sadly saying, "This is all we can do now."

"How can you be so calm? They killed her!"

"They haven't killed her because you are here, and she is you. We cannot interfere with her destiny. With your destiny. But I sent her an energetic force field of strength to help her move through the next few moments. I opened a portal for her to leave and float up into loving light to hold her for a spell. That will help her. She isn't feeling pain at the moment. She is learning. She is safe for this brief moment, being held in the arms of God. Can you see? Over there!"

Kelda pointed a few feet above Lu's head. I could see Lu's broken little body being held by a cloud of light. "When she comes to, she will be in a state of shock. That is where you and I will come in to help her again."

Finally, they were done. She had clearly stopped fighting. She was unconscious. Todd got off of her and pulled her dress back down. The chubby boy had run away when she stopped moving. She came to as Todd shook her. He looked crazed and scared. With eyes that looked both victorious and terrified, he puffed his chest up and said, "Now you know your place, little girl. If I ever see you with my little brother, I'll find you and hurt you again. If you tell anyone about this, I'll tell them what I found you doing to him. I'll tell them that I was just teaching you a lesson. I'll tell them that you're a little slut and a liar, and no one will ever believe you because that's what you are. So, you keep your mouth shut, or I'll shut it for you by shoving my dick in it again!"

She nodded her little head in agreement and rolled over, hugging her tummy. They left her there, dirty, sore, battered, and bruised. Lu got up, found her torn panties, and scooted over toward the bush that was in the corner. She pulled some leaves off of the bush and wiped her bottom like toilet paper.

"Kelda! Oh fuck! I remember this part! My vagina was wet and sticky, and I needed something to wipe myself with, and the leaves worked. They felt cool and soothing on my sore vagina. *I remember that!* Why didn't I remember the vivid details of the assault *until now*?"

"You will soon see why you didn't remember."

I was crying and shaking and experiencing the rape as if it had happened to me all over again. Without asking, I went over and lay down next to Lu. Energetically, I held her in my arms and soothed her. I sang to her a little tune from Bible camp. "It's a happy day. And things are gonna get better..."

She lay there not crying, not weeping, just staring at the foggy blue sky. Vacant like a doll. Every now and then, she would shake. But largely, she just stared at the silhouette of the nails on the blue sky. They were sticking out of the wood planks that were scattered around her. After a little while, she got up.

She brushed herself off as best she could and limped for a few steps, then walked more upright as she settled herself and walked the few yards to the alley gate of her house. Her hair was messed up. She had dirt on her face and on her knees. The ribbon that tied in the back of her blue dress to make a beautiful bow was almost totally torn off. It was hanging off to one side. The bow was still intact but hanging down well past the hem of the dress. She gathered it up and tried to wrap it around her to look okay. She tried to stick it back into the hole where it was torn from. It was hopeless; she couldn't fix it well enough that her mom wouldn't notice the tear. I saw her whisper to herself, "Shoot, my dress tore. Momma's gonna be mad."

"Let's help her here," Kelda said. "Here. Look over there." She pointed toward a dead little bird. "Let's put this into her path so she can find it. This will help."

As she walked inside the gate, she noticed that on the ground to her left was a dead baby bird. It was a little blue birdie. She picked up the birdie and held it, petting it, and a tear came to her eye. "You died, and I didn't, but it feels like I died maybe. I'm so sorry you died. But it's nice, isn't it? Did you fall out of the tree? Did your momma push you out? Did you get attacked like me?" It had already been dead at least a little while because what looked like ants or spiders were making supper for themselves out of its eyeballs and insides. She brushed the spiders off and held the birdie, trying to love it back to life. And then she started to cry.

"Okay, Kelda, I don't remember this bird. I remember the physical sensation of the cool leaf on my sore vagina. I remember the incident with Scotty, but everything associated with his brother has been blank. Why do I only remember bits and pieces of this? It's like a stopgap motion picture movie."

Kelda said, "Yes. Let's keep watching, and we'll help you understand."

She started to cry. She cried and cried until her mom heard her. Julia came out the back door to where Lu was hunched over the birdie. Lu hid it in the folds of her dress and looked up. But she saw it. Julia saw the dead bird. She just made an assumption that Lu was crying about the bird. Lu decided at that moment to whisper to the little bird, "I'll not tell anyone what happened if you promise to live."

Julia said, "What did you say?"

"Nothing, Momma."

"What have you done to your dress? The bow is practically torn clean off."

"I'm sorry, Momma. I didn't mean to tear it. It just happened."

Since Lu often came home with dirty panties, skinned knees, and a ripped dress, she didn't think that Lu might have just been a victim of a brutal attack. No, Julia was too interested in how much work it was going to be with a needle and thread to mend Lu's dress.

"Well, come inside. I'll run you a bath while I finish getting dinner ready. I'm telling you, Lu, you are going to be the death of me. Your shenanigans always make so much extra work for me. I work so hard, and I'm tired. Now I have to sew up your dress, again."

"I know, Momma. I'm sorry. I'll be more careful next time."

Julia didn't even notice the far-off distant stare in Lu's eyes. The stare of a victim. The stare of a being who just encountered something so vile she couldn't even speak of it. As she was walking away, her back already turned and headed back to the house, Julia said, "You've got five more minutes with that gross dead creature, and then it's straight to the bath. I don't want any of that grunge at the dinner table."

"Okay, Momma."

Before Lu went into the house for dinner, she did something that was amazing. She went with the birdie to the wishing well. We watched her stand there as if she could hear something or someone speaking to her. We watched as recognition came to her sweet face. That was when she heard something in the well. Initially, it was a small, almost inaudible voice. Like "Aahhhhh hoe, ahhh hoe." She heard it and looked deep into the well.

"Who's there?"

We watched her face as she saw what appeared to be swirling lights at the bottom of the well. Spirit was calling her... love greater than she could imagine; a presence that makes flowers bloom and the sun rise and fall was calling to her. Spirit calls from the earth, and it calls from the galaxy. It is as great and as wide and as unknown as it is known. This spirit, this love, was calling Lu.

Kelda looked over, put her finger to her lips, and said, "Shh... let's go. It's our time..."

We flew right past her and deep into the well.

What Lu saw was that the lights were iridescent and created what looked like a light-filled whirlpool at the bottom of the well. It caught her attention for sure. She just stared, eyes fixed on the swirling, churning lights while holding the bird in her hands. "Wiluminaaaaaaaa Luminaaaaa!" came from below us. There was a rushing water sound and what sounded like crying. The wind started swirling in conjunction with the lights in the well.

Lu looked a little scared. Her eyes darted around to see if anyone else was nearby. "Are you talking to me?"

And then Kelda started speaking to Lu. "What are you doing with that little bird?" Kelda asked.

"I can't make it live. It's dead. I want to heal it. I want it to live," Lu replied.

Lu was struggling to find words to say. She was operating slowly and stared a lot. She had a hold of that little bird and was staring down at it with hopeful eyes, willing it to live.

Kelda asked ever so gently, "And, sweet child, why is your dress torn?"

Lu replied tentatively, "I am not sure."

"I sense you have pain in your body." As she was speaking, she was slowly, very slowly, ascending up out of the well. She was approaching the little girl like someone would approach a wounded animal—so gingerly and cautiously, for fear that the animal would bolt. I watched with a feeling of deep respect for Lu and for her spirit.

Lu focused solely on the bird and answered, "Uh huh. I guess my bottom hurts a little, and my knees are scraped up …. Those boys, they pushed me down, and they choked me. Everything kind of hurts right now. My back is scraped, too, and it hurts on my bottom."

"Yes, I see that."

Kelda was now in front of Lu. She sat down on the edge of the well. Her body was visible like an orb of light is visible on a dark night. "Bring your little bird and come to me," she said.

Lu asked, "Who are you?"

"I am Kelda. I am your friend. I am here to give you some special powers and strength to heal, and we will heal your little friend there. And in a way, we will heal you too."

She raised her eyebrows a bit. "Powers?"

"Yes. Come and sit near me. I will tell you a little about me. I come from a time and place that you will find is welcoming and healing for you. I come from the past and the future. I come from the heavens and the earth. I come from God, and I come from you. I come from all that is eternal and all that ever shall be. I am the light; I am *your* light. I am the breath of everything that surrounds you."

She looked up at Kelda, her face showing that she didn't really understand at an intellectual level, but that her spirit somehow understood what Kelda was talking about. She timidly said, "Uh, okay. Nice to meet you, ma'am."

Kelda smiled and said, "You can call me Kelda."

"Nice to meet you, Kelda." The sides of Lu's mouth turned up ever so slightly.

"You will go through many learnings, my dear, where you will witness your powers. You are not here to have an easy life, my sweet one. It will be beautiful and magical, but easy? No. You are not here to close your eyes to the oneness of life. You are so young, my sweet one. We did not expect that you would have this first experience at such a wee age. We were not planning to meet with you for several more years. However, you, my dear, have decided to start this journey much earlier than planned. Take a deep breath and let me and my friend scan your body."

As she said that, I became lit up like a light. I was not in the shape of a body, just an orb of light floating next to Kelda.

Kelda looked at me—merely a ball of light floating in the air in a Newport Beach backyard in 1972. She looked at me as if it was the most normal thing for me to be, a floating orb of light, and whispered, "Trust me?"

I looked back at her with eyes the size of saucers—well, if I had eyes, they would have been the size of saucers—and said, "Yes, yes, of course!"

She turned back to Lu. "Lu, dear, do as we do. I need you to just breathe and sit still. Place the birdie on the edge of the well just for a minute. It will be okay there."

Lu followed her direction.

"Now, sit crisscross applesauce and breathe in and out like you are blowing up an invisible balloon. That's right. Good job. In through your mouth and out through your mouth. Create a circle with your breath."

Lu bunched her face up, took a deep breath in, and blew out into the air with her cheeks blown up, too, like a chipmunk. She did this a few times and then seemed to deflate completely. She looked down; I could see her shoulders rise and fall as if she was still breathing in and out. And then she looked up, and in a tiny, tin-like voice, she whispered, "I'm scared... my tummy hurts."

"Yes, I'm sure you are, my dear. You are safe now though. You have gone through something today that no little girl should ever go through. The key element is you *went* through it. I know we just met, but I ask you to trust me. Can you trust me?"

"Yes," she replied in that same tiny voice.

Kelda looked at me and said, "Follow my lead," and we began transforming our light from round orbs into ribbons of swirling light and golden flecks of light.

We began swirling around her. Little Lu experienced it like wind swirling around her. Kelda and I sang in sounds and vibrations. The vibrations permeated her bruised body.

Kelda began, "You were very young to withstand this much pain. Your spirit wanted to float away. But we have great plans for you, my dear. And we need for you to be able to stay here on earth. You will have children of your own, and you will teach others to find their own magic and heal themselves. But first you will need to learn how to heal yourself. We are going to help you do these things. Now, if you trust me enough, I'd like you to follow the sounds of your angels. Follow our voices."

Suddenly there were ribbons of lights and orbs all around us and around Lu, and the most beautiful sound was resonating in our spirits and all around us. *Aaaaaaahhhh hooooe aaaah hoeeeeeedruskahhhhh shaaaaaa shaaaaaaaaaa lom, mmmmmmmm oooooommmmmm shhhhhhhhh sssssssssssssing haaaaaaaaaaaaaaaaaahhhooooe aaaaaaahoe ooooooooooohhhhhh.* The angels sang and covered her in light.

"Lu, it's time to drink from the cup of forgetfulness." Kelda reached deep into the depths under the well, as if scooping up something from way beyond. She raised a transparent glass filled with liquid light. Lu took the glass in her hands, raised it up to her lips, and drank down the liquid. As she drank it, light poured out from her eyes and from the bottoms of her feet and the top of her head.

She giggled and said, "It feels like fizzy bubbles are going through me!"

Kelda smiled and said, "Let's give some to your sweet little birdy friend." The bird still had some tiny bugs visible that looked like a cross between spiders and ants. They became more and more active, moving in and out and through its body. Lu didn't seem to notice them anymore.

I said, "Tell me about the spiders, Kelda."

"At such a young age, it is important for Lu to forget what just happened to her. Drinking from the cup of forgetfulness will do just that. But forgetting has its price, and it is part of her experience. We will set the bird free. It will live. But it will transfer those little spiders into Lu's body. They will stay in her body in her cells and in her tissues, physically reminding her of what she forgot. The body will experience them as physical pain and illness throughout her life. They will stay there, and at times those spiders will become large and hungry. Other times, they will be hardly noticeable at all. But they will accompany her through much of her life. They have been with you since this moment, Lu. I think you know this is true."

"I do. I've never had words for this, but it's absolutely true. Even now, I can feel them inside me."

"Yes, the spider's job is to feed off the sticky, sweet marshmallow feeling that you became accustomed to. Even little Lu, as we see her now, is starting to feel the spiders inside her, helping to shove down the truth. The spiders fill in the hollow and blank spaces created by people who came to steal your body and soul. And when it is time for the spiders to go, because their work is done, Lu will begin a path of recovery that will become her life's mission and her soul contract. Do you recall when that happened?"

"Yes, I recall making a promise to God that what happened to me would never happen to my daughters."

"And you've lived out that promise beautifully," Kelda said. "An interesting fact is that as Lu heals, it will feel like pain. Facing what happened and coming to the truth of her past will cause her both physical and emotional pain. But the pain is a teacher, and it will take you a long time to understand the complete message. Sometimes, you felt physical pain, like your body could recall the trauma and the assault. Other times, it filled your heart with absolute sadness that you thought would last forever. But we know now that the pain never lasts forever.

"Throughout your life, pain was a close friend to these memories. Even when you didn't recall exactly what happened, your body knew, and it shared that knowing with you as pain. It wasn't until it was time for the spiders to leave that you started to remember. Like most people who experience this kind of awfulness, you started to exchange dissociation and numbness for feelings and memories. This served as the signal to the spiders that their time in your body was coming to an end. Without judgment, without fanfare, they began to leave. Now, knowing what you just witnessed, the spiders will no longer take up as much space inside you. And one day, they will be completely gone. The contract we are making with little Lu today will be complete. The spaces and gaps that made up the homes of the spiders will become hollow. You will feel the pain of the empty space as physical and emotional pain in your adulthood. However, as you grow, the pain will dissipate and be exchanged for love.

"As you learn to care for your body and your heart with the full truth, you will receive the gift of integration. That is what this moment is all about. From today forward, Lu, you will live in the truth of what happened and what you survived. There is no more forgetting. The cup of forgetfulness is empty. This truth, while painful, will serve as a beautiful lesson that you choose yourself; you choose to embrace the pain and the joy even with this incredible past. The pain will become your teacher if you do not fight it."

Kelda looked at me with knowing eyes and said, "Haven't you felt that pain in your body recently?"

I took a deep breath and said, "Yes, Kelda! Every day is filled with pain—in my back and my joints."

"Don't be misguided into illness. Let pain be your teacher. Let it teach you how to be more gentle, more loving, and more forgiving toward yourself. The pain will be an example of the healing and the spaces. While they will hurt, they will gradually be filled with the water of life. The plasma we are bathing in right now will permeate the dark spaces and hollows the spiders left. It will take time, my love. This story—no, this gift—is your final chapter with the spiders as constant inhabitants of your body. This story will set you free."

I took a deep breath and simply nodded my head. "Yes."

Focusing back on Lu, we watched her ever so gently pick up her little bluebird. She held it on its back as its little legs stuck up in the air. As she poured a tiny bit of the light water into its beak, most of it fell onto the bird's body. Even though it was rigid from the grips of death, it still had a whisper of life left in it. The light attached to that whisper and flooded the bird with gold. The gold sent the spiders fleeing. The spiders ran up Lu's arms as she watched, her mouth open in amazement as the bird came to life. We watched the spiders enter her body. They swarmed up into her nose as she breathed. They entered her open mouth and poured into her ears. Thousands of little spiders, one by one, marching to their final destination deep in Lu's center. She didn't even notice them; she was so fixated on the bird.

As I watched, tears filled my eyes. It was a joyful and painful feeling all at once. I knew what those spiders represented. I knew the journey ahead for this little one. Focused back on the bird, we witnessed as its little legs started moving. Its eyes closed, and it took a deep breath in. Lu looked up and around with a giant smile. It rolled upright and started singing.

Kelda swooped up the little bird and smiled and said, "You are welcome!" to the little bird.

The bluebird spread its wings and began to fly away—free and well and singing.

"That was amazing how we helped her and the bird through that! But now she won't remember what happened?"

"She will remember parts of it. They will slowly come back to her over her lifetime. The memory will return to her when she is ready to face it, learn from it, and grow."

"These memories then have come back to me now. So that means I'm strong enough to handle them?"

"Yes, my dear, you are strong."

"How did I know what to do?"

Kelda turned to me and patiently said, "You've always known. You just didn't remember."

"Can I go to her and rest with her tonight? I need to comfort her! Can I go and hold her? Please let me!"

"Yes, of course."

"I know that every night she says a little prayer of some sort. Can I help her with that prayer? I know she knows something happened. I know that the pain is still pulsing through her spirit even if she doesn't remember the details anymore."

We moved into Lu's bedroom. It was stark. There wasn't much in it. Since her family was struggling financially, there weren't a lot of extra toys and games and things. But it wasn't the room of a neglected, forgotten child, just one of a child with a family on a strict budget. There were a few stuffed animals and a baby doll, a blanket, and some picture books. There she was on her little twin bed. Her knees were bruised, and her tummy had some very subtle distinguishable bruises. You wouldn't really notice if you weren't looking. But I had seen what happened, and I knew what was there.

"Can you soften the blow of those bruises?" I asked Kelda.

"Yes, my dear; let me see what I can do," Kelda calmly replied. I watched as Kelda bent down and placed her ethereal hands on Wilumina's little bruised body, and the bruising eased. As she was calming the soreness and physical pain in her body, I crawled in bed next to her and held her. I let her know that I was there for her and that I was going to leave her proof by giving her this little prayer that she would grow to depend on each night.

I whispered it into her ear. "Dear Lord, I thank you for this day, and I pray that tomorrow will be even better. In Jesus's name, I love you … Amen."

The prayer was so completely simple but one that a little four-year-old girl could understand. I wanted her to know that there's always tomorrow—or hope for tomorrow. There is always the need for gratitude in our days. Even if we don't understand why things happen to us, when we are grateful and when we understand that every single thing in our world is here to help us grow and evolve as divine spirits, we can say thank you for even the tough stuff.

At this time, Lu did what she needed to do to stay alive. She knew that this experience would not be tolerated in her family. So, she made the decision, perhaps the right one at the time, to put on a happy face and support the needs and hurts of her family and mother. But that icky, sticky taffy that we spoke of in her belly was slowly making a comfortable home for the spiders that now resided in her body.

"Before we go, let's take your sweet prayer one step further. I believe that you are ready for the other half of the prayer. Wilumina, would you mind repeating after me?"

Phrase by phrase, I repeated after Kelda,

"Dear Lord,

Thank you for this day.

I pray that tomorrow will be even better.

Thank you, darkness, for reminding me how strong my light can shine.

May all body memories, mental and emotional wounds, physical wounds, and any contracts of suffering be healed.

May all pain be met with love.

May this prayer heal me.

May this prayer heal my perpetrators.

May this prayer heal the past and the future.

May this prayer heal my ancestors.

May this prayer heal future generations to come.

In Jesus's name. Amen."

Kelda said quietly, "Amen."

What Do Dreams Have to Do with Anything?

I turned back to holding Lu with a new respect and deference for her ancient power and strength. I felt fear for what was coming to Wilumina's (or my) life. But I had knowledge of her experiences as important in her development as a soul and her journey toward changing and shifting her life and the life of her future children.

Kelda let me lie next to Lu, silent and present, until she fell asleep. I must have fallen asleep, too, because I had the weirdest dream. Or was it Lu's dream I was witnessing?

I was in a grassy field. I was dressed in a gown with gossamer layers and ribbon and streams of flowing colors. My hair was long and blonde and held the remnants of a flowered crown. There were others around me, and they were also dressed as if for a party. Many of the others surrounding me were children. I could feel myself in my body, strong and full of muscle. My back rippled with muscle. My legs were strong, and my arms were tense and flexed with exertion, a contradiction to the beautiful gown.

Something was wrong though. We were running and stumbling, and I felt very afraid. But I wasn't just part of the crowd. I was their leader, and it was my job to rescue them. They were with me; I was leading them away from whatever it was that was trying to get to us. We weren't just afraid—we felt terror. What could have happened? I looked down, and I was holding a baby in my arms as I ran. The baby was also terrified, but I assured her we would get out of there. I would deliver myself and her from this horrible place, and we would be happy and dancing again. I said to her, "Just hold on." She understood and held on to me as I ran. Her little nails clawed into my neck and my shoulders. Even though I could see the blood, I didn't feel any pain.

I ran and stumbled. I didn't seem to be making enough progress though. They were gaining on us. I was exerting myself but not really moving, as if on a treadmill. Then, slowly, as we were fleeing our would-be captor, the field started to tilt. It started to break apart, and I was forced to my belly. While I seemed to be able to sense that the others were still around me, the scene got very small and closed in on my own experience. I didn't know where the baby went. I didn't know if she was still with me; all I knew was I was clawing my way over the field. My legs were behind me as if I was climbing or scaling a wall. But I wasn't. I was on the earth, clawing my way through the grass. I was pulling huge clumps of grass out as I went. I could feel my nails breaking and filling with earth. I was still moving but now very, very slow. It was as if each movement took enormous effort, as if I was climbing straight up a hill without the use of my legs. There was a sense that I was holding my breath, but I couldn't really tell. I looked behind me and saw nothing; it was just me on the earth, clawing and scraping, trying to make my way to freedom. And then I woke up.

I opened my eyes. Kelda! She was right there. As my eyes focused, I could see we were back at Sadie's. I let out a deep sigh of relief and wiped the sweat from my brow. My heart was still pounding.

Potato Chips, Bologna, and Sand Sandwiches

Sitting in the comfort of Sadie's porch, I said, "Kelda?"

"Yes?"

"I'd like to visit a fun memory. I know that those rooms down the hall have memories in them. You let me visit a past life, an ancient dance where I think I was the leader. It was so empowering and magnificent. Was that memory another side of the trauma Lu went through?"

"You picked up on that?"

"Yes!"

"When we go through our lives, there is always another side of the coin. It is not often in this life experience, but it exists. Nothing gets past spirit. It is sort of similar to karma. What if we could show that karma was the other side of everything? When we steal, somewhere in our memory of experience on another plane or on this dimensional plane, it doesn't really matter, because the soul knows no separation, but someone is stealing from us. The universe craves balance. The earth seeks balance. If life seems off balance where you are, be assured that in another plane, the earth is balancing things out. Let the universe show you the way. That memory you had with the ancient dance?"

"Yes?"

"It was to show you just how strong you were, and you are. It was a soul retrieval for you. It was a mirror of the power that is inside of you and building inside, Lu. It was a little bit different, but yes, the room is full of memories. Would you like to go see a beautiful one?"

"I would love that!"

You are in control, dear, so think about love, think about what brought you joy as a child, and walk to the third door on your right.

As I reached for the handle, I could already hear the sound of crashing waves. As I opened the door, I could feel the sand under my feet. It was warm from the sun. As I stepped in the room, I could smell dusty sand, salty waters, and the kelp beds of the Pacific Ocean. I closed the door, and a seagull screeched in the distance. I closed my eyes, took a deep breath in, and as I opened them, I was at the beach! I looked around, and it was marvelous!

Our beach town was in the shape of a giant peninsula. On one side was the bay, and on the other was the ocean. When I was small, we went to the bay side. The shore quietly lapped on the sand. There were boats everywhere on that side, creating the only ripple of waves against the shoreline as they motored by. Down the middle were rows of small beach shacks and one two-way highway that meandered up and down the peninsula. On the other side was a giant, wild surf. Huge waves constantly churned and pulsed and crashed toward shore. Both sides had sand, of course. My mom used to take us to the bay side of the beach. This was the memory I walked into.

There were three of us, and we were very young. Maybe I was a bit older now—five or so. I could see my little hands and feet. It was amazing to be back in this small body. The sand came up to the lapping water and then dropped off. We came brandishing old water buckets and Kool-Aid pitchers, wooden mixing spoons, old spatulas, cups and bowls, and used Tupperware that had long ago lost their lids as sandcastle building equipment. We filled our great buckets with water and then dumped them on the sand in order to make it wet enough to build a castle. I smiled from ear to ear. The water was kind of warmish and murky, and as the boats went by, they put out a slight smell of bilge and diesel fuel. *Oh, here comes a boat!* When it got close to shore, we all stopped what we were doing and waved to the passersby. "Hi!" I called out as I waved my hands wildly. "Hi!"

My mom always packed our lunches. Today we had an assortment of sandwiches: peanut butter and jelly and bologna sandwiches, cut into triangles by the big kitchen knife. We each liked different sandwiches, and she knew that. Some days—many days—she was so thoughtful and kind and sweet.

"Mom," I said, hopeful the answer was yes, "do we have any potato chips for my sandwich?" She smiled that smile that scrunched up her whole face. It made the little lines on the side of her eyes crinkle up. She had such a great smile when it went big like that. She had a cleft on her chin, and when she smiled like that, her chin smiled too!

She loved bending the rules. "Don't tell your father. I know it's a bit of a waste of money to buy potato chips that aren't nutritious. But sometimes a little salt and fat is good for the soul."

She handed me the contraband bag of Lays. "Hahahaha!" We laughed as I reached my hand into the bright yellow bag and grabbed a tiny fistful of salty, yummy goodness. I immediately put them into my sandwich. Not only did bologna and potato chips taste delicious, but the chips also masked the crunch of the sand that was ever present and seemed to find its way into every crack and crevice of everything (including me) that came to the beach. She made Kool-Aid too; at first, it was cold and icy and refreshing, but as the day went on, it slowly warmed, and all of the ice melted, and then it was warm and sandy and kind of salty but, in a really weird way, still so delicious.

My mom was there with us in her yellow bikini and not much else. She always had on a sun hat or scarf and the ever-present giant sunglasses. She was so beautiful to me. Sometimes if the weather was cool, she would wear one of my dad's big sweaters over her bikini. And she'd put a towel over her legs. She sat in her sand chair, legs stretched out, tanned skin, always with a book and a glass or bottle of something I knew I couldn't drink in her hand. Sometimes my dad was with us. Today he wasn't. Just me and my mom and my brother and sister. It was perfect.

With that, I took a deep breath and exited the room. I looked up, and the ever-present Kelda was there waiting for me. Tears began pouring down my face. It's pretty amazing to have someone there waiting for you and consistently there to support and guide and love. My love and support had been inconsistent. I knew I had insecure attachment issues. My childhood was peppered with so many bright spots and so many dark spots. I wanted to revel in the bright spots and the love my family had for the ocean a little more.

"Kelda? Can I tell you about another memory I have? I want to talk about things and have someone outside of the memory share them with me. Can we do that?"

"Of course, dear," Kelda replied. "I am here for you. If you need to talk and share, let's do that. Come sit here on the porch and tell me all about it. We have some time and some space for sharing before Lu needs us again. So, yes, now is a good time."

We each grabbed a warm beverage and got comfy on the back porch. I started talking. I needed to talk.

"These memories have brought up a deep longing for my mom. She was the most complex woman, and I knew deep down she loved me, yet I didn't feel safe with her the way I feel safe with you right now. I could never trust that she wouldn't use my vulnerability against me or make it about her. When she died, I had been angry at her for a few years. But now I just miss her, and my heart aches. I'm tired of being angry at her. I want to feel safe to love her again. Can I tell you some more things about her and the beach? It soothes me and makes me feel better."

Kelda took my hand and placed it on her lap. She turned her fluffy couch pillow just a bit toward me and looked at me expectantly, like she was about to hear the most exciting story in the world. It was wonderful.

I began. "The last memory I went into over there..." My eyes darted back behind us to the inside of the house.

Kelda said, "Yes?"

"Well, it sparked these other memories. And I want to share them with you."

"Go on."

"Okay, so as we got older, we discovered my mom was hiding things from us. Wild things. Amazing, unknown experiences that we had no idea were happening so close to our little, quiet, bayside retreat. Other things she hid from us I was unaware of on an intellectual level; I was only a kid. But I knew there were things going on in my mom's life and heart and mind that I did not know about. Now, looking back, I wish I had never found out about them, but uncovering her secret became my quest, all the while learning from her. As I uncovered one of her secrets, I would bury one of mine. I had an instinctual knowing that the world couldn't hold all of the truths at one time. All of this complexity was masked by her ease and beauty and absolute quest for adventure.

"One day, she decided we were old enough to discover the other side of the peninsula. How we got there was just the beginning of the grand adventure. So, she finally let us in on an amazing new treat. This day, we were going to take the ferry across to the bay rather than drive to it from the other side. I was like, '*Wait— what?* A boat that you can drive your car onto? Are you kidding me?' I was literally vibrating with excitement as we cued up in the long line of cars waiting to board the boat.

"Back then, my mom was so cool and so hip—she drove a VW bus. It was light blue with a white top. It had bench seats in the back and a removable plastic floor cover that covered the whole back part of the bus. We never even thought about seat belts! We opened and closed the sliding doors with a giant swing. It often took more than two or three tries to get it shut. Once those doors flew shut, we would wait patiently while my mom got her big purse from the ground. She would heave it up onto her lap and dig around for what seemed like forever until she found her green tube of Revlon plum frost lipstick. She would slowly, painstakingly so, apply her lipstick. Every single time we got in the car, she would do this ritual! Then she would dig around again in her giant bag for her sunglasses, put them on, and back out of the driveway. She would say, 'Beach, here we come!' We'd all shout, 'Yay! Here we come!' as we bounced on our bench seats.

"Sometimes that scrounging through her bag for her glasses ritual would end in a big, heavy sigh. She would turn the engine off, open the door and jump out of the car, go back inside the house, and rummage around for her sunglasses. She'd find them and return after what felt like hours! Sometimes, she'd get back in the car and say, 'I can't find my sunglasses anywhere, kids!' Only for us to all look at her and shout, 'Mom! They're on your head!' Sometimes she'd laugh and say, 'Oh, silly me!' Other times, she would hang her head and take a silent moment. I always wondered what kind of horrible things she was saying to herself during those few seconds of silence.

"Part of her secret world, no doubt. She would wipe her eyes, sigh again, and put the bus in reverse. And we were on our way quietly to the beach. Sometimes I would say, 'It's okay, Mom! We love you!' Or I would say, 'I sure think you look pretty today, Mom.' She would turn around and say, 'Aww thanks, baby girl. Aren't you sweet! What are you kids going to do with a mom like me?' Other times, she would yell at us. 'God damn it! If you kids weren't so difficult to get ready! You were fighting and yelling, and you can never find anything yourselves. It's a wonder I can ever find anything at all. Now we're going to be late to the beach, and we're going to miss all of the good sun because you made me lose my glasses, and now my day is ruined!' We'd say, 'Sorry, Mom. We didn't mean to make you lose your sunglasses. We're sorry. We'll do better next time.' She'd scowl back, 'You'll be lucky if there *is* a next time.' We would ride in radio silence to the bay.

"I loved bouncing along in that bus. Even in silence, under the oppression of fear incited by my mom's bad mood, I still loved it. I'd slide open the windows and stick my head out like a puppy dog; feeling the warm wind in my hair was pretty great for a little kid.

"It's funny, but I remember that every once in a while, after we got home from the beach, my mom would take our garden hose from the front yard, open the sliding doors of the bus, climb in, and simply hose down the whole bus. It was fun to help because the water would spray in our faces and pour out the open doors onto our driveway. Several years later, we had to get rid of that old bus. They said it wasn't worth much. Rust. Hmmm. I wonder what caused that.

"Back to the ferry. I will never forget the first time we boarded the ferry connecting Balboa Island to the Newport Beach Peninsula. It was totally magical, and then the Ferris wheel came into view! We had been driving to the bay side of the peninsula from the mainland, completely missing the magic that was happening at the other end of it. There was a fun zone with a Ferris wheel and a merry-go-round, Skee-Ball, Whack-a-mole, frozen bananas, pinball machines, and photo booths! It was amazing! Magical—like nothing I'd ever seen. I was jumping up and down at the end of the ferry, nearly panting with anticipation about all of the fun we were going to have!

"My mom gave us each a handful of coins, and we played and played for what seemed like eternity until all of our coins were gone. We ran from one game to the next, and as we scored on each game, we were issued tickets that trailed behind us like paper tails. My sister folded hers up and kept them in her pocket lest she lose them. Billy and I loved the way it felt to have the trail of tickets. When all the coins were spent, what seemed like an eternity later, we traded in our tickets for prizes. I got a plastic army parachute guy that, when thrown in the air, would float down to the ground, aided by the parachute. He broke almost immediately but was so worth it. I also got a paddle ball thing that I kept for a long time, quietly practicing the art of a perfect paddle.

"My brother got a yo-yo, and my sister got a bunch of little erasers and pencils and a box of Cracker Jacks. She said the Cracker Jacks were a 'double prize' and worth the tickets because there was a prize in every box, and they were delicious! Thirty minutes later, after we drove our bus off the ferry, we were off to the next big treat! We went to Orange Julius and got these amazing orange drinks that tasted like an orange popsicle plunged into a frosty milkshake. My first thought was, *Ew, gross! Orange juice in milk? Blech!* But my mom said, 'Trust me!' *Oh,* that was a good call! They were so delicious! A symphony of creamy and tangy flavors all rolled up into one amazing cup of heaven! The hamburgers were just okay.

"Then my mom asked us if we wanted to walk on the pier. 'Pier?' I questioned. We went out to the sidewalk and started walking down the street. As we crossed the boardwalk, I was amazed by the show of people all up and down the walk. To my right was a guy with wild long hair controlled on top with a striped sweatband that was pulled down around his forehead. He was roller-skating backwards while jamming out to Supertramp on a big radio he held up to his ear. He had on cutoff jean shorts and a bright green tank top that was cut much too short for my mom's taste. And his shorts weren't just any shorts; they were striped jeans, cut off with the ends all frayed and swaying as he skated (backwards) past us. There were ladies also roller-skating with only bikinis on and nothing else! No cover-ups, no nothing! It was outrageous!

"I was fascinated by this amazing and colorful scene. There were people everywhere, lounging around, listening to music, and laughing. They were all up and down the beach. Since we were walking on the pier and not on the sand, we were able to see everybody lying around for miles. It was a hot August day, and Newport Beach was having a heat wave. People had umbrellas set up everywhere, and I couldn't keep my eyes off the lack of clothing! At our little bayside retreat farther north up the peninsula, most people were modest. My mom was the most beautiful and alluring mom on the beach. Here she struggled to maintain her cool demeanor. I noticed as her gaze followed the men and women up and down the beach. She had on her white daisy dress and yellow bikini underneath. That day, she was wearing her scarf around her head like a kerchief, and she had on her ever-present giant sunglasses and frosty plum lipstick. To me, she was a supermodel! I wonder now if she was a little intimidated by the showiness and a bit jealous of the recklessness the young people showed, parading up and down the boardwalk and lounging by the sea.

"There was so much happening. We walked and walked for what seemed like miles to the end of the pier. My mom loved the pier. I don't know if it was because it was up out over the ocean or what, but she always loved to walk to the very end. My brother went nuts with excitement.

"When my mom died, my sister and brother and I had a private ceremony for her at the end of the State Beach Pier. Oh, Kelda, thank you for helping me remember this very special time!"

"I can tell that you had enormous love for your mom. I can tell that she loved you too. People are often blinded so much by their own pain that they miss the pain being experienced by the people in front of them. In your mom's case, she was fighting a battle inside that you and your siblings had no part of, and yet somehow, you became the casualties of that war. If only people could understand that the very first step to any healing is to turn inward and learn to love and heal themselves. We can only love others in the same capacity we love ourselves. And if, as in the case with your mom, someone has such an enormous buildup of self-hate like she did, it makes it impossible to see the world through any other lens. Her ability to see you and your siblings was tainted by her own pain. It was never about you. Do you understand that now?"

"I do now. Is this part of the reason that I'm here now? So that I stop repeating these patterns with my own children? Oh my God, am I too late? Have I hurt them the way my mom hurt me?"

Kelda looked at me crossly and said, "Now you know damn well you haven't raised your kids in the same way. Lu! You've hurt them in your own special way." She smiled and slapped her knee.

I nudged her shoulder and said, "Kelda!"

We both laughed.

"Okay, okay—I get that I've been a different kind of mom. A more accessible, reliable, and consistent mom. But I've had so much pain filtering through my system. They're bound to have felt much of that pain."

"Yes, they have. But we are here to teach you, and ultimately them, that the key to everything is to understand we are all connected, and it all starts inside one's own heart. People get so busy trying to save the world while ignoring their own needs. Truly, if you save your heart, then you will save mine. Remember the tree? The branches or arms of God? We are all connected. When you heal your heart, you heal the world. Speaking of healing, little Lu's light is on. Are you ready to give her some support? Remember the love you feel for your mother. Understand her pain, and let's support Lu through the eyes of love."

Frogman Tubs

We came to the scene through a wall of light. Lu was saying defiantly, "Mom, I don't want to go." She was eight or nine years old. Her mom and dad were struggling in every way. Nancy, the nanny who had lived with them, left when they moved to a new house. I had vague memories of her. She was a kind woman who cared for us. She lived in the back room next to the garage, and in the summer, she had parties for us with clowns and games. But she was gone. My mom and dad were trying to make things work. As was the theme and the constant in our home, things were difficult and trying for them, especially for my mom. My mom, who couldn't see past her own pain and suffering enough to care for her children, was at her wit's end. She was exhausted from working and having to keep up the house and care for my sister, brother, and me.

Even before my dad moved away, he was always gone; he always had evening meetings at work, and of course the weekends were his main workdays. She was trying to keep everything afloat. But how do you keep a ship afloat when you're drowning? Frank had stepped in when the nanny left. We had been spending quite a lot of time with Frank as of late. He oversaw maintenance at the church and had taken a special interest in the three of us over the last few years. Frank wasn't married and was socially awkward. He wore small, round glasses and had perpetually wet lips. His face was oily, covered in pockmarks, and the color of Silly Putty. His hair was greasy but long, and balding in the back. He combed it all back into a long, scraggly ponytail to cover the balding, but there was always a patch of scalp in the back that he couldn't cover with his greasy, combed-over hair. When the sun would hit his bald patch just right, you could see that there was a divot in his skull. It would pool with sweat and oil and become shiny. His hair always smelled of grease and hairspray. He was tall and skinny, but even with his skinny arms and legs, he had a big belly. When he wore his work coveralls, he looked kind of like a hairy frog to me.

At this moment, Frank had generously offered to take us kids for the weekend so that my mom and dad could reconnect. My dad had scheduled a substitute pastor for his church, and they were going away for a reparative overnight somewhere lovely. I knew this because my mom had shared her joy and excitement about it the whole week leading up to it.

Being the preacher's kids, we had grown accustomed to being pawed at, hugged, squeezed, and kissed by the parishioners at the church. My mom and dad would tell us that if we rebuffed their affection, we were rude. I would stand there, stiffen up, and allow the little old ladies and men to kiss and hug me. I took what they gave me, week after week. Often, the offense would be a wet cheek. The little ladies would either lean down or pull me to them and kiss my face, always smelling of dime store perfume, Ponds cold cream, and some kind of bar soap. I'd have to wait until they walked away to wipe the sticky spit off my cheek. Or they would tap my nose or ruffle my hair. Sometimes they would make me sit on their laps. This abuse, this lesson in not saying no lest I hurt their feelings, was reenacted every weekend after every Sunday service, potluck, meeting, or event I was part of at my dad's church.

Putting up with Frank's advances was just something I thought I had to do. He was very "affectionate" with me. My mom used to say how sweet it was that Frank liked me so much. That I should feel special and honored. He would come over in the evenings and read to us. My sister and brother would sit by his sides, and me, well, I had to sit on his lap for story time. His big belly pressed against my back as he read us books. The *Velveteen Rabbit* was a favorite of his. It was confusing for me. So confusing. I was starving for male attention since my dad was never home. I was also starving for affection since my mom always seemed to be too tired or upset or moving too fast to make contact with us. It was nice. We really loved Frank. That is, until it was time for him to leave. He would pucker up his big frog lips and kiss me. In the beginning, he would kiss just my cheeks and leave a big, wet mark. It was yucky but no yuckier than the other old people and parishioners who felt they had a right to completely violate my personal boundaries of space and safety, all under the watchful eye of my mother, who would scold us if we recoiled in any way. Even now, looking back, those first years were okay, I suppose. But I had an uneasy feeling about Frank. Why didn't my sister or brother feel it the same way?

Back to the weekend. By this time, Frank had become a constant figure in our lives. While my dad was at work and my mom was away, he would take us out to lunch or the movies. Sometimes we went swimming at his apartment. On special occasions, he would take us to Knott's Berry Farm or to Disneyland. We would have fun. Then, like clockwork, as our time came to an end, he would reach down and kiss us. His once questionable kisses started to become more aggressive with me. He started kissing me goodbye on the lips. Those big frog lips would envelop my whole little mouth and leave a wet, sticky, smelly imprint. I hated it.

On the days we were with Frank, my anxiety would build as the day wore on—waiting for the moment when he would do something that made my stomach turn. He had also taken to giving me piggyback rides, a lot. Jumping up and down with me on his back while he reached behind and held me up. He would bounce me up and down with his hands cupping my bottom. He would play "tickle torture" with me and my sister and brother. Mostly me. I remember when the "back rubs" started. He would give me back rubs and then ask me to rub his back. Since I was hungry for attention and affection, I would let him. He would say a little rhyme as he rubbed my back. "X marks the spot, a circle and a dot. Tight squeeze, ocean breeze, now you have the chills." As he said this, he would trace a big x on my back, circle my back with his fingers, and then poke me with his finger for the dot.

He would then squeeze my neck or my sides and then blow on the back of my neck and run his fingers one more time down my back. At first it seemed okay. It tickled and felt kind of good. I did get the chills. But then he kept wanting to play that game more and more. His behavior continued to escalate. The weekend of my parents' big getaway, I didn't want to go.

Frank showed up to our house with a big smile on his frog face, bubbling with excitement. My sister and brother were happy and excited too. It was Saturday, and we were going to have a sleepover and swim, swim, swim. Frank's place had big sliding glass doors that faced the big apartment complex swimming pool. Our plan was to sleep on the floor in sleeping bags in his living room. My mom had our bags packed and our sleeping bags rolled up and waiting by the door. For some reason, I felt sick and scared and anxious. So, I did what a normal kid would do: I begged and pleaded with my mom to not have to go.

"Please… I'll be good!" I wouldn't bother her and my dad if they would only let me stay home. I didn't have the luxury of comprehending what personal boundaries or space meant. I had long before lost the ability to dissent against invaders in my space. I didn't understand why I felt so scared and so anxious. I didn't have the vocabulary or ability to say to her, "You're sending me to be with a pedophile. You are placing me in the arms of a predator." No. All I could say was that I didn't want to go and I didn't like him anymore.

Well, Frank overheard my "temper tantrum." He heard me say I didn't like him and that I thought he was gross and I didn't want to go. My mom left me sobbing in my room and went to attend to him.

"Oh, Frank, I'm so sorry. I don't know what's gotten into Wilumina. She's so difficult and has such a stubborn, selfish streak. I'm so sorry she's acting like this."

I heard him say, "I understand. Yes, Wilumina is a bit of a wild one. She's feisty, and that makes her special. She needs to be tamed. I will help you with that if you'd like. She needs to understand that I'm only here to help her. Maybe it would help if I went and talked to her?"

"Oh yes!" she said. "Frank, you're such a dear man. What would we do without you?"

He came into my room and sat down on the edge of my bed where I was lying down on my tummy, by this point whimpering. He put his cold hands on my back and said, "Wilumina, this isn't fair after all I've done for you and for your family. You're hurting my feelings. I have grown to love you. It hurts that you don't love me back. What have I done to deserve this? Why do you hate me? I've only ever wanted to be your friend. Your mom is tired, and you're making it worse for her. I only want to help you and help her. We've had a lot of fun together, haven't we? Listen, sweetheart, I will try harder to be nicer to you, and if I've done anything to make you feel unloved, I am truly, truly sorry. I love you, Wilumina."

Before he left, he swiped his hand down my back, to my bottom, to the edge of my dress. He then turned his hand and continued to ever so slightly swipe his fingertips down the inside of my thighs to my kneecaps and walked out of the room.

I had no words. I felt guilty and bad and sick and scared. Was that normal what he just did? Was rubbing my back like he did normal? Maybe it was. I didn't know. I was a fucking child. So, what did I do? Well, I filled my little brain and heart up with questions, doubting my own judgment and questioning my feelings. Why was I being so difficult? Why was I making such a fuss? Maybe I *was* spoiled and selfish. We had done a lot of fun things! I simply said to myself, "Okay," and began crying again into my pillow.

Then my mom came back in. She sat down on the bed and leaned forward and whispered in my ear. "How dare you embarrass me like this. Frank is helping me, and he's helping your daddy. You have hurt his feelings, and you have humiliated me. You get it together, little girl. You stop this right now and go with him. If he decides to stop helping me because you can't seem to figure out how to think about anyone else but yourself, I don't know what will happen. I can't take it anymore. I need a break, Wilumina. *I need a break.* I'm going to count to three, and you are going to get up, wipe your face off, straighten your hair, smile sweetly, and apologize to him. You are then going to take your suitcase and your sleeping bag and get in that car with your brother and sister and go have fun with Frank."

As I was starting to get up and wipe the tears from my face, my mom made sure to seal the deal by saying, "You think you're special. You think the world has to cater to your needs. What about my needs? Do you think it's easy being your mother? Do you think I'm having a good time? No! Sometimes we have to do things we don't want to do. You have no choice; you have to go. Your selfish behavior is exhausting me, and it's hurting this family. Why do you think I'm so tired all the time? You! You make me this way. Why can't you be more like your sister and brother? They don't give me such trouble. I will only say this one more time." And very slowly and quietly, she hissed, and as she said it, I could feel her breath on the back of my ear, "Listen to me carefully, baby girl. You will go. You have to. You will apologize." Then she raised her voice loud enough that it made me jump.

"Now!"

I got up, and I wiped off my tears, and I smiled sweetly, and I apologized to Frank for hurting his feelings, and I went. That weekend, my sister and brother slept in sleeping bags on the floor of Frank's living room. I slept with him in his bed.

"Kelda, I can't tell you how much these experiences shaped my self-worth and my value. I was faceless. Just an object of affection. I learned that this is love. I did that by shutting *me* down. Instead of taking care of my own needs, I lived through the lives of others. I feasted on the souls and the pain of the people around me in order to find identity.

"Damn, Kelda, I even became a therapist. My whole life was about listening to and helping other people because I surely couldn't help myself. How could I, after being taught so well, so clearly, so efficiently, and so succinctly that my feelings, experiences, and pain were not to be expressed or to be voiced but to be churned and pulled and stretched like marshmallows on a taffy pull for others? I had no value other than being what other people needed me to be or do for them. And this caused a fire in my belly to heat up from the rage and pain. It melted the taffy marshmallow and turned it into goo that stuck to my bones and still doesn't want to let go.

"This pain never left me, and those same spiders that were blown into my very being a few years earlier munched and crunched and chomped and lived off the goo and sticky taffy that symbolized my feelings. Everything in my life conspired to silence my voice and keep me from speaking up about what was going on inside of me."

Kelda said, "How does this make you feel about your mother right now, Lu?"

"It makes me sick to my stomach, and I feel full of rage and sadness. How does someone forgive their mother for offering up her child to such a person? What on earth possessed her to do such a thing? Why couldn't she see what was happening to me? How could she have been so blind to the abuse I was sustaining under her watch? What was going on in her heart and in her soul that she didn't protect me from such a monster?"

Quietly, Kelda looked at me and said, "And yet, you want to forgive her?"

The truth was, this adult version of me knew that her lack of caring for me wasn't about me. I knew that she simply didn't have the ability to see past her own pain, and this made her blind to the pain her own child was going through.

"Lu, you know your mom was a complicated person. She had her own demons that she fought with all of her life. There was one moment in particular that sealed how she chose to look at the world forever more. Would you like to see the moment that caused your mother to become the person you knew as a child?"

"Oh yes, Kelda. I would very much!"

Julia

"Come, let's head back to Sadie's." She looked me in the eyes and said, "Water is the way."

I replied, "Nothing but love," and began to feel that now familiar vibration that came with the particular kind of traveling we were doing—the rushing sound of water and the blackness that turned to light that I was beginning to trust. When we arrived at Sadie's, there was a nice spot on the porch and two cups of cocoa already waiting for us.

"When you are done with your cocoa, the third door on the left is waiting for you. Inside, you will find some answers about your mom."

We sat together in silence for quite some time, enjoying the space and sipping cocoa. When I was ready, I took a big breath in and out and centered myself in love. Then I got up and walked from the back porch through to the hallway of doors to the third door on the left. As I walked in, it smelled like an old movie theater.

Salty and sweet, popcorn and candy. It was a small room. On one side of the room were bean bags and pillows. On the other side was a big movie screen. It took up the expanse of the far wall. There was a bowl of popcorn and some Red Vines on a tray on the ground next to the pillows. I plopped down on the pillows and bean bags, grabbed a Red Vine, took a few bites, and settled in to watch the movie. I was very curious and more than a little apprehensive. Most of my experiences in the rooms so far had been intense.

The film started playing, and my mother, Julia, was the star. She was in her brand-new apartment. Julia had just completed her first year of nurse's training. She and three of her friends rented a tiny apartment off campus for their second year. This was her first time living away from home, a home where she had shared a bed with her single mother for most of her teen years. Julia was thrilled. She had grown up in a very strict house. Her father died in the war, and her mom never remarried. Her mom, my grandmother, was as strong as they come. But she was very quiet and reticent in her ways. Julia was none of those things. She was bright, loud, beautiful, and rebellious. Rebellion came easily to Julia. Her mother, Caroline, was a dedicated follower of a very strict evangelical church. Caroline was a faithful parishioner. Faithful and observant. She did not allow drinking, junk food, or soda. No music unless it was hymnals from church. Especially no rock 'n' roll. No movies. No radio. No makeup. No dancing. No sex outside of marriage. No exposed shoulders or kneecaps. No dating. No boys. No fun.

To Julia, this was torture, and she rebelled in as many ways as she could. Nurse's training was one of those very acts of rebellion. Julia wanted to make a living and get out of her momma's house. She wasn't going to wait until she found a man, got married, and then moved out. No, not Julia. She was going to be an independent woman!

When she moved into an apartment with three other girls, it was huge! She had never felt more *alive*! The only problem was that she had to share a room with Shirley, but at least she had her own bed. The girls each had a twin bed in separate corners of the room. They also had three drawers in the dresser Shirley's mother donated to them and a little desk to work at. It was perfect! The roommates had a strict rule that no boys could ever stay overnight. No, this apartment was for girls only.

Julia loved the days when she could be home alone. Not that she didn't like her roommates. She loved them. She felt so grown-up just to say she had roommates! It was just that with four girls in the house, well, it was a pretty busy place. Julia was on her break from classes and had come home to make a sandwich. She promised herself that once she was done with her sandwich, she would definitely get started on reading for her anatomy class. "Catch a Falling Star" by Perry Como was joyfully playing on the radio in the kitchen. It was a warm California day. Only the screen door was closed. Julia felt alive, and truly, she felt for the first time like she was going somewhere. She was finally living!

As she sat there listening to the radio, a handsome traveling salesman came to the door. He knocked on the screen door—*knock, knock, knock*—and then said in a cheerful voice, "Anybody home?"

Julia froze in the kitchen.

"Hello?"

Damn. Why did she play her music so loud? Her mom always taught her to lock the front door and never answer when a stranger was knocking. She had raised Julia to be extra careful of strange men. As a single mom, Julia's mother was in a very unique situation for the 1940s and 50s. They always had a No Solicitors sign on their front door. Those darn traveling salesmen with their vacuums and encyclopedias! They didn't even open the door to the Avon lady when she came to the door "Woo-hooing" and saying, "Avon calling!"

Julia thought her mom was nervous all the time—about everything. Silly things too. Julia's response to her mom's strict guidelines for life was to mock her and make fun of her devout nature. Julia thought the church's rules and her mother's rules were silly.

When the Avon lady would call through the door, Julia would think, *Certainly Jesus would want us to have a little fun! Momma, you're just no fun.*

But eventually, Julia would say, "Come on, Mama! Have a little fun! Try on some lipstick!" to try to goad her into it.

Caroline would sheepishly respond with, "No!" and "Don't you know vanity is a sin?"

Julia would roll her eyes and say through the door to the Avon lady witnessing their banter, "Sorry, ma'am. We only decorate our faces with the love of the Lord!" Sometimes Julia would quickly stick her head out the door and say, "Leave me some samples and your card in the mailbox, and I'll call you later. Thanks!" before slamming the door and saying, "Bye!"

Julia turned the radio in the kitchen down a bit and set the apple she had been cutting on the counter. And listened.

"Hello?" he said.

"Um, miss, I'm pretty sure you're home! I really need some help. Hello!"

He was speaking through the closed, unlocked screen door.

She heard him test the handle.

"Miss, I'm so sorry, but I need to use your phone. I'm in a real jam. I gotta sell these last three vacuums by tonight, and my car won't start. I thought I could make it to my next appointment before running out of gas, but darn if I was real off in my mileage calculations. Hello? Miss?"

Julia took a deep breath and thought, *Well, he knows I'm here, and I don't want to be rude.* She answered, "Just a minute!" as she gathered herself and walked out from where she had been hiding in the kitchen. At the door was a very nice-looking, handsome man in a business suit. His hat was in his hand, and he needed help. He had run out of gas. Julia thought for just a moment how silly her mom was, how she had raised her to be so scared of everybody. Especially men. She didn't want to go through the world as scared as her mother, and here was a person in need of help.

So she went to the door, and through the screen door, she said, "Um, hello. Tell me again what it is that you need?"

And the salesman said, "I'm so sorry to bother you, miss, while you're enjoying your music on such a lovely, sunny day, but I have run out of gas, and I just need your phone to call the tow truck to take me and my car to the nearest gas station down the block."

He chuckled and said, "Don't you know, I'd walk there myself, but it's just so darn hot out."

It is hot today, Julia thought. *The radio person said it might top ninety degrees today.* Julia then noticed that she was dressed only in a loose house dress and was hardly presentable to a gentleman she wasn't acquainted with. She pulled together the lapel of her dress and slouched her shoulders forward in an attempt to hide the fact that she was braless.

"Also, could I trouble you for a glass of water? I've darn near sweat through my suit coat. Do you mind?" he asked as he began to take off his suit coat.

"Oh my, yes. Where are my manners? Please come in, instead of standing there sweating in the doorway. The phone is right there in the parlor. I'll just run to the kitchen and grab you a glass of water." Julia showed him where the phone was by the couch. She turned toward the kitchen to go get a glass of water, humming to herself the tune of "Catch a falling star and put it in your pocket."

When Julia returned with the water, the man wasn't using the phone. He was just standing there smiling at her. The look in his eyes had changed from friendly and grateful to one of a wolf in hot pursuit.

She also noticed that the front door had been closed and the deadbolt locked.

"Ahem," she said, clearing her throat. "Here's your water." She set it down on the coffee table. She noticed that the man had something shiny in his hand. His breathing had changed. It was slightly shallow, and his face had begun to turn a little bit red. *Is that a knife?* she thought. The man was not smiling anymore. Julia took a deep breath and said, "Oh God."

She closed her eyes tightly and said a quick prayer to herself, Deuteronomy 31:6, *"Be strong and courageous. Do not fear or be in dread of them, for it is the Lord your God who goes with you. He will not leave you or forsake you."*

When she opened her eyes, the smile returned to his face. He had stepped a few steps closer. She could smell the sour smell of his sweat and a vague smell of cigarettes on his breath. He took another step closer, and just as polite as could be, he said, "Now. Miss, could you show me where your bedroom is?"

Julia ducked quickly and ran back into the kitchen. She went to grab the knife that she had been using to cut the apples when he first knocked at the door. While Julia's mom always taught her to be cautious, she never taught her how to fight. As she got to the kitchen, he stepped in front of her just as she got the knife in her hand. He grabbed her hand with the knife in it and twisted it behind her back, cutting Julia's hand in the process. She let out a halting screech. She was surprised at the lack of sound that came from her throat.

He put the hand that was holding his own knife over her mouth and said much less politely, "If you want to live, you'll shut the fuck up." She could feel the blade on her cheek. He had her other hand, the one that was bleeding, twisted behind her back. He came behind her, moved his knife to her neck, and said, "Now, miss, would you be so kind as to show me where your bedroom is?"

Julia was unable to produce any words. She just nodded her head up and down, crying and gasping, terrified into submission, frozen in place.

He demanded, "Show me!"

He gave her a little shove, and Julia started to walk toward her room with him breathing down her neck. When they got to the door of Julia's room that she shared, he saw the two twin beds.

"What is this?" he asked.

"This is my room. That is my bed."

He threw her onto her little bed. He pounced on her. Biting and licking her. As he started pulling off her panties, he realized how small the little bed was, so he threw her to the ground facedown, knife to her neck.

He said, "If you make any sounds, I will kill you, I swear. I cut you. I will cut you again."

Julia hardly noticed, but the blood from her hand was everywhere. Everything flashed red. She could feel the knife press to her neck. She could feel it starting to cut at the soft skin right under her ear. She could smell his breath on her hair, and she just thought, *Stay alive, stay alive, stay alive.* His tie was still on, and he was fumbling with his pants. It was hard for him to get access to her on the floor, so he picked her up and threw her back on her bed, her torso on her bed and her knees on the floor, and he laid on top of her and thrust into her.

She screamed another soundless scream, and then she went black as he thrust and thrust, robbing Julia of her innocence, of her sense of safety, of her sense of self, of her sanity. Something broke in her that day as he tore into her, biting her back, biting her neck, pulling her hair, thrusting and thrusting. It was taking so long. When would it end? Julia left her body and went somewhere else. As he split her body in two with the force of his rage, he broke her. She was shattered, a thousand tiny pieces of her scattered to the wind, never to return. He was having a hard time staying hard, so he pulled out, turned her around, and thrust his penis in her mouth. He thrust, and she choked and gagged and nearly vomited. He threw her back on the floor. Snot, spit, and tears were pooling now in Julia's ears as she lay back and he penetrated her again. This time, he thrust until he came inside of her. There was blood everywhere when he was finished. Blood from her hand, from her mouth, and from her vagina.

He said, "Look at this mess you made! We'd better clean it up before your friends get home!" He got really close to her. He held the knife back up to her neck and said, "If you tell any of them about me, I will come back, and I promise you, I will fucking kill you, and then I'll fuck all of your friends and kill them. I know where you live. I know your name, and I will fucking kill you." Still wearing only his shirt and tie, he went into the bathroom, grabbed a hand towel, and brought it to Julia so she could wrap her hand to stop the bleeding. The cut was pretty deep. He said, "You'd better get that looked at. It might need stitches." He pulled on his pants and left the room.

Julia lay there for a while. Or it seemed like quite some time. She thought, *I must clean up, I must clean up. There's blood every-where. What will they say?* That's when she heard the man. He hadn't left. He had gone into the bathroom and turned on the shower.

He walked back into Julia's room, looking around as if surveying the room. Julia found her voice to say, "I think I need to go to the hospital. I think I need stitches in my hand."

He said, "What you need is a shower."

He walked Julia with a towel wrapped around her hand into the shower. As she stood there frozen, confused, and shaking, blood running down between her legs and on her face, he very gently unbuttoned her dress and helped her into the shower. He turned the water to scalding hot, and he washed her body. He scrubbed the blood off her legs while she raised her cut hand up over her head. He then left and took her dress and the sheets and a com-forter and a little rug at the foot of her bed and put them all into a big trash bag. He mopped the floors and cleaned off the walls where her blood was splattered. He returned to Julia, who was crouched in the corner of the shower, shaking. He reached in and turned off the water, picked her up out of the shower, and put her terry cloth robe on her. He walked her to her little bed and gently set her down.

Julia looked up at him, and she didn't know why, but she thanked him for cleaning and running a shower for her.

"It's the least I could do." As sweet and as kind as could be. He then picked up the bag with her bedding and her dress and blood in it, went into the front parlor, and grabbed his hat and suit coat. He straightened his tie and smoothed out his hair. The man tipped his hat and said, "Miss, it's been a pleasure." He unbolted the door, turned, and walked out.

Julia let out a breath and began to wail. And then just like that, she sat up. She got new sheets and a blanket and set them on her bare little bed. She put on a new house dress and went to the kitchen. The floors were clean, no more blood, and the knife that she had been using to cut the apples was washed and neatly set on the dishrack. He had cleaned up everything.

Her hand was still bleeding. She needed to fix that. Julia was in nurse's training, so she and her roommates had butterfly bandages and gauze on hand. They took turns practicing tending to make-believe wounds on the weekends.

She treated her hand. She thought maybe it might need a few stitches, but the butterfly would be okay. Once she felt like her hand was pretty secure, she went back to her bed. With one hand, she did the best she could to make her bed. She noticed there were just a few little splatters of blood, so she wiped the blood off the walls and a few spots that he missed off the floor. And then she just went and sat on the couch, her hand in the air, mended but still bleeding. She still had a towel around it as she sat there humming to herself, "Catch a falling star and put it in your pocket," rocking back and forth until her other three roommates came bounding in from class and found her there.

"Oh my goodness, Julia! What happened!" they shouted.

She said, "I cut myself." She was in shock, which was why she was able to say it so flatly. Her roommates thought of it as calm.

"I cut myself," she said again.

Her friends looked at her cut and said, "We think you need stitches! Here, let us help you!" The three other nursing school students got to dress a wound for real this time. They were so excited to help her that they didn't really notice that anything else might have been askew.

She repeated her story. "I was cutting an apple, and I cut myself." As far as Julia was concerned, that brutal attack never happened, and Julia never spoke of the visitor.

And the film cut to black.

In present time, I realized I had been squeezing and twisting one of the pillows so hard that a seam had ripped and some stuffing was coming out. I dried my tears with the stuffing and then quietly stuffed it back into the pillow. As I hid that pillow under the others, I hoped no one would notice that I had accidentally ripped open a pillow in heaven—or whatever this amazing place was that kept revealing my past to me. Some place between here and there, in Sadie's house, this magical gap in time that revealed so much.

When I felt ready, I returned to Kelda, who was still sipping her cocoa as if no time had passed.

She gently looked up. "Hello!"

"Hi."

"How are you doing?"

"Um, okay, I think. Kelda, I didn't know that happened to her. How could she move forward after that?"

"I believe she moved forward the same way you did, my love. She did her best to forget. But the body never forgets. The traumas and the pain break through in destructive ways. For your mom, this shifted something in her. It changed her. It changed her very nature. It took her ability to see other people's experience away, and it blinded her to others and their pain. Your intuition about her being blind to your pain was correct, Lu. This experience, or the reaction to it, clouded her perception of everything else in her life. It didn't take away her love. But it took away her ability to see past her own pain. It created in her a myopic view of the world, and a single point of view emerged. From this day forward, everything for her was sorted and sifted through the cloudy, murky lens of her own pain. She never recovered. Sure, she found love, and she experienced joy and happiness many times in her life. She loved you. I want you to believe that and know that without question."

"It's funny, Kelda. I've always known that. I've always known that she loved me. I've also always known that I fell into her blind spot, and she never really saw all of me. She couldn't have. Otherwise, she never would have done what she did. And I forgive her. With all my heart, I forgive her.

"As a child, there was an implicit agreement in our house that my mom's pain was more important than anybody else's. I knew that I wasn't allowed to express anything about the marshmallow taffy pull in my belly or the spiders my own trauma planted there to feast. The only way from it was denial. It was all my parents knew. There was also an implicit agreement in the house that I was responsible for helping her through her pain and shoving down my own. As I did this, my body became comfortable with the resonance of that energy so that I could continue to be responsible for the needs and desires of others—most importantly, my mother's. And if someone else hurt me, I believed it was my fault."

"It was a perfect recipe for someone like Frank to take his place in your life," Kelda said. "Shall we go back to your experience and continue?"

"Yes. I'm ready."

Why Is Frank Still Here?

I said to Kelda, "For years, Frank treated me like a girlfriend. Frank would say I was special to him. That was what was confusing. He took me and my brother and sister to help my mom out, but he always took a special interest in me. He even took me away on weekends to visit his friends. He'd drive me around in his big Ford truck, and I felt so special. For Christmas, he bought us fancy gifts. And he made me kiss him. He'd talk to me about his life and his problems and his loneliness, and I'd eat it up. He told me how special I was and how pretty I was. He took special photos of me and my mom. He took photos of my sister and brother and me around the pool and pictures of my sister and me in our swimsuits, posing seductively for him. Why did he do that?

"When I'd rebuff his kiss, he would act hurt. And when I didn't want to go to his house anymore, I got in trouble. Why is it when I hear certain songs, I get that taffy pull feeling in my stomach? We used to go to his apartment and spend the night. We went swimming a lot. There's a feeling I get even to this day; I can't wear a wet swimsuit. It does something. It gives me a weird feeling to feel the wet cloth and smell the smell of chlorine. The wet cloth of my swimsuit is oozing with taffy and marshmallow. Why is that? Why don't I remember? Why does that experience make me feel so sick?

"What grown man has a seven-year-old girlfriend? From seven to twelve, that's how it was. We went on vacation, just the two of us. The subtle and insidious perpetration and boundary violation was the exact diet I had been groomed to eat. Later in my life, I told my mom that I thought that Frank had molested me, or at the absolute least, he had emotionally molested me. A seven-year-old girl is not a grown man's girlfriend. You do not force a seven-year-old girl to kiss you. You do not tickle torture a seven-year-old girl until she cries, while pinning her down and tickling her. You do not touch a seven-year-old girl on her shirtless back with 'X marks the spot, a circle and dot. Tight squeeze, ocean breeze, now you have the chills.' You are a grown man—you don't get to do that to a little girl and then be hurt when she feels uncomfortable. When she feels like her voice is less important than your need for companionship, it's simply not right. No part of it was right.

"I often wonder what my mom and dad were thinking. Were they so checked out? Years of emotional and physical molestation. And when I was grown and told my mom, she said, 'How dare you! You were a handful; you were really difficult. I needed his help. Why do you think you went to camp so much? You were too much.' She sent me off with a pedophile because I was too much. It was my fault. So I ate her pain and shoved mine down. I ignored my pain and swallowed hers so she would feel better. The truth was, when my mom felt better, I felt better. It was a direct correlation. I adored her. I'd do anything for her. I would even go with him to please her. This pattern of responsibility for men, for people, really shaped my experience. It even included the natural curiosity that grew about my own sexuality and how I was to be sexual to please others. It was never a question of my own pleasure; sex was for others, not for me. I was a shell of a person as I got older. And this affected everything."

As I sat there with Kelda, I was aware that I was full of anger and rage. I felt a deep grief going through those memories. We flew through them in our conversation, but they had not taken place over a short period of time. Frank had been in my life for years. Years of molestation. Kelda and I had visited only some of the experiences. To help me understand what?

I felt like a victim. I was angry at everyone. I wanted to get out of the pain and confusion of my early childhood years. I wanted to lash out. But as I looked at Kelda, she and I both knew we still had a long way to go.

Safe and secure at Sadie's house, she took my hand and said to me, "My dear, you are reexperiencing these traumas without the cup of forgetfulness so that you can learn, relearn, and then rewire your reaction to your traumatic truths. These traumas live in your very DNA, and we have to rework their hold on you so we can let them go once and for all. I wish that you'd experienced only one or two, but what you have been through is complex. The myriad of insults to your body, heart, and mind have created an intricate and complicated web of reaction. Sometimes you rescue and take full responsibility for things that are not your own. This is met with buckets of self-doubt, self-hatred, self-abuse, neglect, and abandonment. You have no road map to do it any differently because your mom had a version of the same story. A different cast of characters, but many of the same responses, so she never taught you any other way.

"I want you to see now, as an adult, that there are different truths than the ones you accepted so long ago. By taking time to revisit these memories, with distance, compassion, and maturity, you can reinterpret these traumas and reinterpret the people who harmed you. Then you can start to move to the real work: forgiving yourself. We understand that you have forgiven them. You get a gold star for the forgiveness of others. My dear, it's time to forgive you. It's time to really understand you."

"Why now?"

"Because now is the time. Many people get this review at the end of their life. Most of the people around us have completed their lives and are doing their reviews completely in the rearview mirror. Some are deciding how they want to return to earth or who they want to be when they return. Others, who feel they have completed their learning, are free to move on to other universes or other spheres of existence. If someone is contemplating returning but feels like their time as a human is done, they may be considering returning as an animal to cohabitate with humans as guides and angels. Some recognize that they still have lessons to learn because their time spent here wasn't well lived. Perhaps their spirits were too fragile, or they got too lost on their journey and need to go back with an easier assignment. For example, they may need to learn more about cooperation, so they will return to earth as an ant or another simpler creature to live out that lesson.

"Others, like me, are spirit guides. Spirit guides inhabited the earth thousands of years ago for a little while. But we now serve in a different way. You may think of us as angels or entities that empower higher wisdom to serve all. Our role is to guide you. You and I have been connected for a long time; our connection is ancient, Lu. You are also a healer. Right now, your guides are here to help you heal your own past, which ultimately heals us too. Your life has been about healing the scars and conflicts of the past. You are learning now how to live differently so you will stop perpetuating the same traumas that you and your mother experienced. You're doing this so you, your daughters, and your daughters' daughters have a different life, one free from the insanity you and your mother both experienced in far too many ways.

"It is as if the cosmic buck stops with you, if you can learn these lessons well enough. We weren't necessarily expecting you right now. But, Lu, you have been full of surprises since the day you were born. Rarely do we get the opportunity to do this kind of review halfway through a life. But here you are, my dear. And I'm so honored to walk with you.

"To get to the core of it, the bottom line of all your struggles is denial of self—a supreme denial of your own right to love yourself. A strike down. An annihilation of the right to your own experiences in this body you have been given."

I turned to her, lifted my eyebrow, and said, "Well, I see why people don't do this until the end of their lives. It's fuckery."

We both laughed until our eyes brimmed with tears, and then we returned to the silence. Though I wasn't speaking, my mind was racing.

A young woman walked into the room with a plate full of little pink and white circus animal cookies and two more steaming cups of hot chocolate. I looked at Kelda and teasingly said, "You guides sure like sugar!" The young server handed the plate and cups to Kelda, who was sitting next to me holding the plate in one hand and the two cups in the other.

Kelda said, "I'm happy to take them away."

We both started laughing as I said, "Don't you dare!" We sat in silence for a few more minutes, drinking the most delicious hot chocolate and eating my favorite cookie of all time. I turned to see her face full of serenity and purpose, thoroughly enjoying the little pink elephant. I was getting used to this look on her face by now. It let me know that she was about to drop a truth bomb on me.

I shifted in my seat a bit, looked sideways at her, and said, "What?"

She cleared her throat and then said, "Wilumina, understand this, my dear. This will put things into a different perspective when we go through these next memories and experiences that you have endured."

I replied, "I understand that I learned early on that being an important part of my family meant denying who I was. But I'm here now. I'm here."

Kelda seemed to be preparing me. "We are going to do some more time travel soon. It will be forward to another part of your experience that shaped you."

Kelda began speaking to me about my life, telling me what I already knew but not in this clear, succinct way. "Wilumina, these next two experiences we are going to visit shaped and molded not only your internal world but your external world as well. This is where you learned to stay quiet with men and not assert yourself, or else they would hurt you. You learned that your worth was predicated on your ability to be darling and pleasing to get attention. And if you couldn't get attention for anything else, then you made the decision to get it this way. It makes sense, right? It was the safe route, the known way. During this time of your life, your mom and dad fought like cats and dogs. Do you remember how you used to sit outside their room and listen?"

I looked down and nodded my head in agreement with the memory. "I wanted to save them," I said. "I thought I could help them work things out. I would go to them both and try to comfort them. My mom cried a lot. She started drinking a lot around that time. All the while, every Sunday, we would dress up as a family and sit in the front row, smiling and listening to my daddy preach. Then, once we were back in the car, the fighting or crying would start again.

"As I think about it, we didn't play together very much as a family. We mostly bonded over pain and recovery from some shouting match. My mom's focus was on diving into her pain or running away from it. She was so much fun. She would do and say things that would have you rolling in the aisle with laughter, and just as quickly, she would be crying."

Kelda, taking a deep breath in, said, "It was around this same time that your mom was diagnosed with bipolar disorder."

I answered, "Yes. Yes, it was. I learned to understand her moods based on what music she had playing on the record player in the living room. Her favorite musicians were Barry Manilow, Judy Collins, James Taylor, Carly Simon, and Carol King. She played their records a lot. I knew that she was in a good place when I came home from school and 'Copacabana' was playing. We, of course, loved it when she was a little manic. Sometimes she had gone shopping, and there would be bags of clothes all over the living room floor. Or she had sewn new outfits for my sister and brother and me, never sleeping the night before. She would dance and sing and swing us around, and she would be marvelous! She'd tell us stories about her 'hippy days, before I met your father,' living in LA, near Verdugo Hills and Mulholland Drive. But if I came home and she was listening to James Taylor or Judy Collins, she would be in her bed or on the couch, crying and angry. She would either yell at me for not doing my chores and being lazy, or she would ask me to lie with her and hold her while she cried. She would sing 'You and Me Against the World' and 'Where Have All the Flowers Gone?'

"I would crawl up in her lap and let her stroke my forehead and the side of my temple and sing softly over my head. I would feel her breath as she sang, and the words rustled the strands of my hair. Or I would try to hold her and let her snuggle with me, usually until she fell asleep. In both scenarios, her ever-present two best friends were by her side—Ernest and Julio Gallo. She drank that jug wine constantly and always on the rocks in an iced tea glass. Soon after that, she was hospitalized for bipolar disorder and alcoholism."

"How hard it must have been without your dad there."

"It made it infinitely more difficult for all of us."

"Want to talk about it?"

"I'll never forget the day he left. We all went to the airport that day. My mom and dad had created a verbal cease-fire to make the trip and departure more pleasant for us. The other times they declared verbal cease-fire agreements were on Christmas and sometimes on our birthdays. Because we were all smiling and Mom and Dad were being kind to each other, I knew this was a big deal."

We watched as the screen of my father's departure unfolded in front of us.

We all drove together in the big blue VW bus. My brother and I were bouncing along in the middle seats, and my sister sat sullenly in the very back. She was not going to pretend that this was just another fun adventure. Our dad was leaving. My mom and dad sat in the two front seats. My mom was driving for some reason, and my dad sat upright and very still in the passenger seat.

My mom was wearing one of her best outfits. She had on a blue dress that tied at the waist. To match her dress, she had on frosted blue eyeshadow and frosty pink lipstick. Her hair was permed and fell in curls around her face. She had on her big sunglasses that hid almost the whole top half of her face. My dad had on a navy blue suit, white shirt, and burgundy tie. It was his outfit. He usually wore that or some facsimile of it most days. He had purchased a straw hat for the sun earlier that week. He held the hat on his lap. On the floor next to him was his hard-sided briefcase. It slid forward and backwards as my mom drove us all to the airport.

They were speaking to each other in short, curt sentences, not really making eye contact. My mom was watching the road as she drove, and my dad was finding very important things to look at through the window. I was right behind my dad. I was paying close attention to both. If they looked back, I would quickly turn my head and pretend I was also watching very important things pass by us in the window. I saw her look over at him a few times and then say nothing.

And then finally I heard her say, "Tell me again—when will you arrive in Tokyo? And then how much longer until you arrive in Cambodia?"

Dad replied, "It will take about twelve hours to get to Tokyo. I will then change planes and fly to Bangkok. I will stay in Bangkok for two weeks while I acclimate and learn about my mission to Cambodia. I will be on the ground in Phnom Penh in about two to three weeks."

"Okay, okay," she said. "Tell me again—why you are doing this?"

"Julia, we've been over this. I had a dream that I needed to go to a foreign land and save the people who otherwise would never come to know about the love of Jesus. I've been called to be a missionary. I'm needed in the squalor. There's no place for me here. I need to go save the children. I can't just sponsor them anymore. I need to go and save them. You don't want me around anyhow, Julia. I've been sleeping on the couch for months. You've wanted to be free from me for years. You get to divorce me free and clear. A new start for everyone."

"When I said I wanted a divorce, this isn't what I imagined," she said, looking at him sideways as we approached the freeway on-ramp. The bus lurched forward as she punched the gas. I also lurched forward. I caught myself with my hand on the back of the passenger seat just before I hit the floor. Neither seemed to notice.

"Me either, Julia. But when the Lord speaks to you, you must answer. I am his humble servant. I must do my part for the Lord. I must spread the Gospel far and wide. That's what I was told in my dream. When this missionary position just fell into my lap, I knew it was a sign from God. It's my destiny."

"What about your children?" she pleaded.

"What about them? They'll be fine. They have food and shelter and clothing and a country not at war anymore. They have schools and a capable mother and all the things they need. They don't need me."

"But…" she said, her words fading as if they had fallen off a cliff.

"But what?" he asked.

"Nothing," she said. "Who can argue with God?"

We drove in silence for a few minutes. Then she said, "Okay. Tell me again—when will you be back?"

"For the thousandth time, I don't know. A few months, a few years. Come on. We said we would be happy about this."

Mom swallowed a big gulp, took a deep breath in, and said, "Yes. This is for Jesus." She pasted her church smile across her face.

After that, they sat in silence for what seemed like a long while. We bumped along on the freeway to the airport in the farthest right lane. The bus shook and trembled when it went over sixty miles an hour, so my mom stayed to the right while the other cars zoomed around us. My brother was curled up in his seat, reading a Calvin and Hobbs book and twirling a little piece of his sun-bleached hair at his temple. In the back, my sister was lying on the bench seat and appeared to be asleep.

I was as alert and engaged with them as ever—an uninvited observer and guest to the end of their marriage.

I started to speak to Kelda about what I saw. "Even though my mom and dad weren't speaking, there was still so much going on between them. I learned that if I stopped trying to look at people with my regular eyes. and I looked at them from my mind and senses while I sort of unfocused my regular vision, I could see people differently. I could see tendrils of energy swirling back and forth between them even though they were silent. They were still in a heated exchange. Lost in their own thoughts, they were unaware of what their energy was doing."

We watched as the energy between them flailed and struck and retreated in their exchange. All the while, they sat up straight and stiff, my mom's eyes on the road and my dad's out his side window.

From the back seat, they were unaware of how intently little Lu was watching them now. She leaned forward, sitting on the edge of the scratchy vinyl seat, bracing herself with her foot on the underside of her dad's chair. There was a small piece of edging cord that had worked its way out of a seam at the front of her seat.

"I remember that thread scratched my leg each time we turned."

Then Lu moved in even closer. There weren't seat belts back then, so she moved as close as she could. It was clear she was deeply engrossed in the battle going on in front of her.

"It's weird to be able to see people's energy," I began. "It's something that at first kind of scared me. But over the years, it has been helpful. I think we can all do it. But it's hard to see people in ways other than with our eyes. It hurt me to see them like this. This unspoken energy war."

We heard Lu start to pray silently, "Dear Lord, please take my mom and dad's pain away." Her effort to change the energy in the car was unsuccessful, so Lu took a different tactic—pure distraction.

She cleared her throat. "Daddy…"

"Yes?"

"Daddy, I'm really happy for the children in Cambodia that you're saving. They need you there, really bad, Daddy, don't they?"

He turned in his seat a bit to answer. "Yes, Lulu, they need me a lot. But more than me, they need Jesus."

"Yes. Yes, they do," I said.

He went on, "We have so much here, and they have nothing. I am going to help them understand that Jesus is the answer and that when—and only when—they turn to the Lord Jesus Christ as their personal savior will they be free."

"But, Daddy, the little boy on the refrigerator looked more like he just needed food. Isn't that what he really needs?" I asked.

For years, our family sponsored children from all over the world. We had their photo and a little bio about where they lived and what they needed. They often had little flies on their faces and swollen bellies. I learned that their swollen bellies weren't because they were full. Their bellies were swollen from being hungry.

"Lulu, we will be providing food as well as the teachings of the Lord Jesus Christ. We are spreading the gospel across the world. Praise be to God," he answered.

Lu scrunched her face a bit and said rather non-enthusiastically, "Praise be to God."

We heard her say in her thoughts, *What about us?*

"Kelda, I was always trying to find the positive side of things in my family. I was the self-appointed peacemaker. I would try to soak up their pain into my little body and then give it to God so that they could feel better. It often left me tired and feeling weird or sad inside. I believe I've done that my whole life with many people. I think I learned at such a young age to do that because if I could diffuse the situation and get others around me to feel better, I would in turn feel safer. I've had to unlearn this as I've gotten older. It's not healthy for me to constantly be soaking up people's pain and trying to transform their feelings. I've learned to put better boundaries around who and when I do this with people. But at the time, it was a valuable survival tool."

As they pulled up to the airport, we heard Lu's dad offer one last reassurance that "the church will make sure you're provided for." Which was true for a few years. Mom nodded her head up and down absentmindedly.

"Okay. Okay," she said, that same smile pasted on her face.

"Kelda, the truth is that as the years went by, the checks slowed down, and then they stopped coming altogether. In the years to come, I would hear my mom on the phone trying to get through to my father.

He seldom called us. He moved around from country to country. We never really knew where he was. He did send postcards from time to time. I would bring them in for show-and-tell. 'These cards are from my daddy! He's out saving the poor people for Jesus!' I would say.

"I'm sure his absence added to my mom's depression and exhaustion. She was on her own. No child support. No communication. No help from anyone else. That is except for Frank. He was always there to 'help.'"

We watched as they got to the airport and walked inside as a family one last time. The kids and mom all hand in hand, dad a few paces in front. At the gate, they waited in silence until his flight was called.

"Flight 345 to Tokyo is now boarding."

Then, just like that, he picked up his hat and put it on his head. He bent over and very slowly picked up his hard-sided briefcase. Hat on head and briefcase in hand, he kissed both girls on the top of their heads and gave his son a hearty handshake.

"Kelda, he nodded to my mother. He didn't dare touch her. It was so surreal. We stood in a line at the window, watching him walk onto the tarmac, climb the stairs, board the waiting airplane, and go out of our lives."

Kelda replied without words. Words weren't needed. With her knowing and loving eyes, she looked right into my heart. It was such a wonderful feeling to be listened to from the heart and not just from a place of intellect or discussion. She heard me, and for once, I felt safe. I felt held. I felt supported.

The Turn

"Kelda," I said, "are we headed to the years that felt almost too much to handle?"

"Yes," Kelda said. "Yes, my dear—that's right where we are going."

"I feel like I need to preface this a little bit. Maybe not necessarily for you but for me. I need to get a little perspective on what I did and how I acted. I was a little wild!"

Kelda said, "Yes, perhaps you were, my dear, but there is no room for shame here. Tell me what you need to say. Say it all. I want to hear about all of it, Wilumina."

"Thank you for hearing me the way you do."

"It is my honor to listen to you. Please begin."

"I became aware of my body shape as I got to be about ten or eleven. I had forgotten the trauma of the alley, and a lot of my friends were older than me. I had begun to use food as a coping mechanism for the chaos in my home, and I started to put on a little weight. From sixth to eighth grade, I gained weight. I also hit puberty. I remember I was tallish then. Not the tallest but tallish. I was getting curves and feeling excited and repulsed by them at the same time. I wanted to be small. I got picked for the volleyball team in eighth grade, and I got put on the C team. The C team, in my mind, was all the big girls. It seemed as if they picked the teams based on size. The smaller girls were on the B team, and the big girls were on the C team. That could have been the case or just a coincidence; I don't really remember. Perhaps the bigger girls were the better players. Who knows? And by *big*, let me say these girls weren't big girls. They were taller and stronger, and I was one of them. Why I felt insulted, I don't know. I guess it went back to the idea of what beauty was, and to me, that meant being small. I didn't want to be heavy and big. But I was big. The problem was the boys started to notice me, and I felt important. I liked it. I wanted their attention. But at the same time, it felt yucky. I felt like they were looking at my body, something that I felt was gross, and they were saying, 'Hey, baby, I like your butt.' It was so confusing.

"I was just thirteen. Thirteen! I had no direction. No rules around sex. No one ever talked to me about sex. No one talked about anything. 'Just don't do it' was all I heard. 'And if you *do* do it, then you're bad.' I was overwhelmed about starting high school and feeling so young and not ready. So, I fell into a new group of friends who were doing what my family labeled as 'bad' things. For the first time, I felt okay. Being with them felt more like home than my home. With them, I was accepted. They liked me, even with my big body and all of my quirky ways. I felt loved.

"My new friends talked a lot about having sex. I was totally not ready. I had only kissed a boy or two, and I let one other boy touch my boob behind the library earlier that year. Other than that, I didn't know anything about sex. Up until this point, my sex ed teachers had been three boys who assaulted me and a grown man who seemed to think I was his special love interest. My father was silent on the matter when I was younger, and now, being gone, he was even more distant and silent. Even my now single mother who was dating everyone in the book kept her mouth shut about it. I often dug through her drawers and found sexy love letters written to her from men and different kinds of "massagers." Sex was something she was having but not a topic we ever discussed. It was assumed that sex was something I knew nothing about. That is, until I met a boy who was older and seemed to like me."

Kelda interrupted me. "Lu needs us again." On the wall, the little red light was lit up to let us know that Lu was going to need us soon. I knew what was coming. I wanted to stall.

I took a deep breath. "Wait, Kelda. Isn't there something we can do to help support Lu? I gave her the prayer of gratitude. Can we give her something to love? Something she can hold on to before we dive into this part?"

"My dear, don't you remember? I gave you Carrie," Kelda said sweetly. "Or rather, I placed all of the love of the universe deep into that little bear's stuffing, just for you."

"I remember I did have Carrie Bear. Carrie Bear? *Oh* Carrie Bear! Yes! I got that teddy bear in kindergarten. I got it for Christmas. I carried that bear with me everywhere. Kelda, I'm a grown woman, and I still have that bear. When I lived overseas, people would say that your belongings went into three categories. Stuff that you were okay to say goodbye to if they got lost, like your furniture or mattresses and things like that, went into a shipping container. Other personal items that you held dear, but, truly, if they were lost, you'd feel sad, but you'd live—these items were packed in a suitcase and went on the plane with you. And then there was the carry-on bag. In that bag were the things you couldn't live without. I always put that teddy bear in my carry-on bag. I still have it, and if I'm having a really bad day, I might even sleep with her.

"Her magic is from you?" I asked with a big grin.

Kelda giggled and said, "She is from Santa Claus."

"Ha! Santa Claus!" I smiled.

Kelda went on. "Truthfully, the magic that lives in her came from me *and* from you! Her purpose was to teach you how to love, without the yuck of your past. Her little bear nature taught you love because, Lu, love comes in all forms, and you needed something truly unconditional. If you're still sleeping with her now, it seems to me that it worked."

I looked at her and, with a heartfelt breath in, said, "Thank you!"

Kelda took my hands and said, "Water is the way…"

I took a deep breath in and started chanting, "Nothing but love. Nothing but love."

"I am glad you are feeling loved and supported and ready to face some other experiences that you have successfully blocked from your conscious memory. There are some things that need love and forgiveness. Are you ready, my dear? Or do we need to go back to Sadie's and take a rest?"

"I'm ready."

I took a deep breath. I filled my heart with love and connected to the earth and to the sky as I breathed.

"Water is the way," I repeated. "Nothing but love. Nothing but love."

If Only I Could Float Away

"Water is the way" and the response "Nothing but love" felt like a ritual from church. It felt holy and sacred. The secret code words to move through worlds and time and space… through the darkness and into the light.

Kelda and I walked into what looked like a party. We were at a party. Or rather, Lu was at a party. She was so young, yet she was tough and had an edge about her. She looked ready to prove to anyone at this party that she fit in. Anything to escape how empty and alone she felt at home. Being a part of this bad-ass crew made her feel good. They were happy and always joking, the complete opposite of her home life. She wanted to be a part of this group. So she walked with a swagger, laughed at all their jokes, and drank cheap beer to fit in. She smoked clove cigarettes that made her lungs hurt. She wanted to be one of the cool kids.

Lu was leaning on a tall boy named Chip. He was a football player and a "bad boy." He had come from another school and was a year older than Lu. This was the party where people were taking turns going upstairs and "doing it." Lu and Chip were up next. Everyone around Lu was laughing, and one of her friends said, "Have fun!" as they left the main room and the crowd. Walking down the hall, we could see the swagger in Lu's step fade away. They passed another couple, and Chip high-fived the guy. Lu looked at the ground, trying to hide her nerves. As they entered the bedroom, Chip started to kiss her and pushed her down on the bed. She reacted with a fake laugh to hide the quickening of her breath. She didn't want him to see how scared she really was.

They kissed a bit more. He knew it was her first time, but he had little patience for her. Her virginity was just another notch in his belt. So, instead, he said, "You know they'll want a full report, so we better get on with it. If we don't, I'll look bad. You like me, right?"

"Yes."

"You don't want me to look bad in front of my friends, right?"

"No."

"So, let's lay down and…" He paused, as if thinking what to say next. "Yeah, just open your legs a little bit."

Lu reluctantly said, "Okay, but would you rub my back first?"

I looked at Kelda and said, "Oh my gosh, that's what Frank did. He always rubbed my back."

"I know…" Kelda said.

"I didn't even put that together. How come I asked him to do that when I was so disgusted with Frank when he did that?"

"That's what grooming is, my dear. You were primed for this from a very early age. You literally didn't know any better."

"My God, Kelda. Did I ever have a chance at this not happening?"

"Not at this moment. This is part of what the cup of forgetfulness did. To help you forget the alley, you lost some of your connection to what was truly dangerous for you. Instead, you connected to what was familiar. And since Chip was like Frank, asking him to rub your back felt normal."

"It's so wrong…"

"I know…"

I leaned over, put my head on Kelda's shoulder, and sighed. Kelda gently touched my head as we turned back to the scene in front of us.

We watched as Chip took off her clothes and rolled her over on her tummy. He sat on top of her bottom and squeezed her shoulders a few times. Then he kissed the back of her neck and got up, saying, "Lu, roll over."

Feeling shy and timid, she rolled over and pulled the covers up to hide her body. "You know I can't get in there if you don't pull those covers down."

She looked at him without moving, her eyes pleading with him to stop this but not having the words to say, "Stop."

"What's wrong with you?"

She whispered, "Nothing."

"Good. Now spread your legs."

Lu didn't move.

He took a plastic packet out of his pants. He tore it with his teeth and one hand while he stroked his penis in the other. Then he rolled a condom over his penis with both hands.

Noticing she hadn't moved, he placed his knee between her legs and said, "I said, open your legs. Don't you know what you're doing?"

"You know I don't," she whispered, barely audibly.

"What?" he said.

"Nothing…" She braced for what she actually *did* know was coming next.

"Come on, Lu, relax! I thought you were cool."

As she started to reply, "I…" he kissed her hard on her mouth and rolled on top of her.

Her body went limp.

In response, he said, "There—that's better," taking her lifeless body as consent rather than what it actually was, which was total terror.

There were no questions about how she was or if she felt ready. His attention was solely on himself; he barely even looked at her.

As we watched, we witnessed Lu leave her body.

As he thrust into her young body, Lu wasn't there. She had already floated away.

"Kelda, I remember this moment. It felt oddly familiar, and I didn't know why. Now I know that I had been here before. In that alley, I learned how to float away. I remember it hurt, but I wasn't really there. The floating away part was what I focused on. That emptiness felt familiar. It made me feel calm."

We could see her staring to the side with an arm shading her face. She was intermittently holding her breath and trying to take little gasps of air in the spaces when his body slightly lifted.

We could see she was floating even higher. His body completely consumed her. He was a big kid. There was no space between his body and hers. As he thrust with his whole body, her limp body moved under his. How was she able to even take a breath? With the weight of his big frame, he didn't even notice that his chest had pinned her head sideways to the bed.

When the rocking stopped, it seemed to be an invitation for her to reenter her body. We watched as most of her spirit came back. But an interesting thing happened: some of his dark spirit mingled with hers, blocking her spirit's full reintegration. His darkness entered her energetically and barred her from parts of her own soul… and the spiders feasted.

He rolled over and lay next to her in her friend's little twin bed, smiling a great big smile. He gave her a big kiss, but he didn't ask her how she was. He just smiled so big. So she smiled back. They lay there for a minute in silence. Then he did something that startled her. He cupped his hands around his mouth to make it look like a megaphone and shouted, "Yeah! Woohoo!" really loudly so everyone downstairs could hear. Then he said, "Get dressed! We gotta get downstairs so someone else can do it now." He got dressed faster than she did and ran downstairs.

She went to the bathroom. She sat on the toilet for a moment, just staring. She started to pee and grimaced because it really stung. She very slowly and methodically rolled the toilet paper over her hand, right hand over left, wrapping her hand in toilet paper. She wiped herself and slightly shivered, flushed the toilet, and just sat there for another minute. Then she took a deep swallow of air and jerked her head back as if steeling herself. She stood at the sink but didn't dare look in the mirror. She couldn't face what she saw. The room seemed to close around her. Instead of facing what had happened, what it did to her, she concentrated instead on the suds she was making with the soap. Watching them as if there could be answers for what had just happened. Looking for clues in the bubbles.

She exited the bathroom, and we watched as she took deliberate steps—right, left, right, left—down the hallway alone. As she descended to the main floor where the party was still going on, all of his friends looked up at her and started clapping and high-fiving him. She looked white as a ghost. Part of her did ghost out that day. Part of her died inside. But instead of crying or leaving, she shoved her pain down to fester in her gut, giving more food to the feasting spiders. Instead of feeling it, she relished in the badness of it. Pasting a smile on her face in an effort to hide her true feelings, she dramatically rolled her eyes and asked her girlfriends for a beer and a clove cigarette. She laughed aloud, acting cool and proud of herself.

"Oh my God, look at your hair! It's all messed up on one side! Like, you guys totally did it!" They all seemed genuinely happy for her.

Wishing now she had looked in the mirror, Lu quickly ran her fingers through her hair, "Yeah," she said. "It was totally awesome."

I said to Kelda, "I remember that night so clearly. I just shoved it all down and added it to my other sticky marshmallow feelings. It was a few months later that I stopped eating. I walked out of that house a changed person. I was humiliated, and yet I belonged. I stayed with that boy; he was my 'boyfriend,' and I let him violate me over and over again in the name of what I thought sex was supposed to be. I thought it was my duty. Nowhere had anyone taught me that my body mattered. It was for men to use. It continued that way for decades.

"At thirteen, I had just barely started my period. I hadn't fully developed yet. I was tall, but my breasts had not yet filled in. I was a little bit chubby around the middle, something that happened to lots of my friends. But unlike some of them, I was very aware of my shape and how to evoke attention. It was through my body. Everything was through my body. It was my gift to others. It was the place where men had full reign. I was not supposed to say no. I was not supposed to fight or kick or scream. I was supposed to be quiet and get through. The only way I could deal with it was by floating away. The truth was I liked the feeling of leaving my body. I liked the feeling of floating. The only way I knew how to do that was when men were abusing me. As painful as it was, it also brought me a sense of peace and safety that I didn't know in any other places in my life. As strange as it sounds, it was in the pain that I felt safest because when the pain came, I could float away.

"Chip taking advantage of me was the first time I remember the feeling of floating away from my body. In that moment, I learned that through pain, I could also find an escape—one that I so desperately needed because so much of my life was so hard.

"You know, Kelda, people say to watch out for sexually transmitted diseases. I say watch out for sexually transmitted demons. In my life, the number of demons I had to face felt real. Very, very real. But let me tell you, in hindsight, the biggest perpetrator of my life was me. I wish I could say that it was my mom or the litany of boys who objectified me. I'd like to say that they treated me terribly. Some really did. But what happens next in the story isn't about the men who abused me or the mother who neglected me; it's about how I abused me. It all started a week or two after Chip broke up with me."

It's Impossible to See through Pain-Tinted Glasses

Lu had a little journal where she used to write her feelings down. She didn't keep much, though, because she was scared her mom would find it and read it. This journal became the voice of her demon.

"Yes," said Kelda. "Let's go to her now. Water is the way."

"Nothing but love." I felt a sensation of not moving down into the past but moving sideways, like through a film projector on super speed fast-forward.

There she was on her bed, writing down something. It must have been the weekend because she was wearing a swimsuit.

Kelda and I had entered the room and were sitting at the foot of her bed. Lu was writing something down and had a big frown on her face. She looked intent and scowled. I peered over her shoulder to see what she was writing. I must have gotten too close because she suddenly itched her face and looked behind her. Kelda, who was standing back a bit, looked at me and gave me a little "easy does it" hand motion.

I looked over her shoulder again and saw what she was writing. She had doodled in the book pictures of rats. Rats everywhere. And in between the rats, she wrote:

You are a fat rat. You are nasty and dirty, and you crawl around in the night like an infestation. You are fat and gross. You have dirty, greasy hair, and your breath stinks like garbage, and you are fat. Fat rat, fat rat, go eat some garbage. All food is garbage. All food is disgusting. You are disgusting. I do not allow you to eat. You have lumps and bumps and rolls like tumors, you troll.

"Oh, Kelda! It's so cruel." I began to weep.

She held my hand and said, "Let's go rest. Water is the way, my dear. It is always the way. Follow your tears and remember, nothing but love."

I repeated, voice cracking and my nose running, "Nothing but love, nothing but love, nothing but love," and together we returned through the darkness and the light back to Sadie's house.

As we settled and I took some deep breaths, I continued as if no time had passed in getting from there to here. "I kind of remember this part of my early teen years. I remember feeling power and a strength inside I had never felt before. It felt good to be so cruel. How strange that the perpetrator was me, and also the victim. The rescuer was in there, too, I suppose. I inhabited all three.

"Kelda, I've had a hard time going back through these memories. They've opened up pain. I think about and feel angry about why my mom wasn't emotionally there and my father just left. Kelda, why didn't they protect me?"

"My dear, I am not their guide. I don't know their karmic lessons or debts. But I do know that you are with them, as God says in the Lord's Prayer. 'Forgive us our debts as we forgive our debtors.' Perhaps they were not here to protect you but to teach you forgiveness. You have learned over the years self-protection, have you not?"

"Yes, Kelda, I suppose I have. It's been a journey."

"Wilumina, might you want to take a rest? I believe there is an important message for you. When you are in a rested state, you can hear it more clearly."

"A message? Yes, I need all the messages I can get at this point."

"Take a rest here, my dear."

I lay down on what was perhaps the world's most comfortable sofa ever! The fabric of the pillows was *the* softest velvet I could ever feel, and the stuffing was like clouds. I instantly felt comfortable, held, and at ease. As I was lounging and resting, I felt a slight tickle on my forehead. And then behind my ear. I lifted up my hand to scratch my hair. As I did, my hand felt like a disembodied hand petting my head. I had a sudden surge of sadness as well as sweetness. Tears came to my eyes as I stroked my forehead. I knew at that moment my mother was there with me. I felt her near me. I felt the weight of her sitting next to me. I could smell her and feel her. I didn't want to risk not seeing her, so I kept my eyes closed. She said to me as she patted my head, "I didn't know. I didn't know. I'm sorry."

"How could you have not known?" I whispered.

"I was too wrapped up in my pain. I couldn't see you. I couldn't see anything but pain. Honey, I am so sorry. Please, please, please forgive me. I love you with all of my heart. I also didn't know what you know now, about the divinity of others and the divinity of my own being. I had so much to learn in this life. Thank you for being a kind of guide for me. Thank you for teaching me and loving me. Thank you for fighting for us, for fighting for your ancestors and for striving to face the pain and love it back to life. I didn't know. I didn't understand. I was battling against everything.

"You have taught me, baby girl, through your brave living, that there is no battle. There is only love. My sweet girl, I am sorry. I am sorry. I am sorry. I didn't know. I love you. I have learned. I am here now. I will not leave. I will be here with love, honor, and respect for your being and for your bravery. I still have much work and learning to do, and so do you. Stay in love. Stay in faith. Know you are held and cared for and supported. All of it is for this. All of it for you to understand and to transcend. All of it is for you."

I must have dozed off because the next thing I knew, Kelda was sitting next to me.

She turned and said, "Lu's light has turned on again."

I took a deep breath in and then exhaled twice as long, looked into Kelda's kind eyes, and got up and followed her.

"Where to?" I asked. "Or should I say *when* to?"

Kelda laughed and took my hand. This time, we just dove into the light.

Little Pink Houses for You and Me

We entered a scene back in Lu's bedroom. She was fifteen. She was now living on Melaluca Street again. She was so, so thin. Her bedroom was simple, yet it had some pretty touches. It looked like someone had decorated it with intention. It was wallpapered in small pink flowers. There was a desk with a little bookcase on the side. It was painted white. The carpet was brown shag, and the drapes covering the sliding glass doors that led to the backyard were shabby and much too long for the window. A thin, oversized pink bedspread covered her twin bed that sat in the middle of the room. The bedspread was too big and was bundled around the bottom of the bed. From her door, there was a long hallway that led directly to her mom's room.

I turned to Lu and said, "We moved so much back then. We lived here more than once. The house was on a cul-de-sac and across the street from my mom's best friend. I think my mom wanted us to move back to a place we had known before. We moved pretty much every two years from the time I was born until I was well into adulthood.

"Sometimes we had to move because our lease ran out. Other times, we moved because our money ran out. Sometimes we moved because our luck ran out. It happened so often that eventually my mom would leave some of our boxes packed and just throw a cloth over them with a small glass topper and use them for end tables. I got really good at decorating my room in a jiffy. I hung that wallpaper myself. I found the bedspread at Pick 'n Save and painted my desk white. I needed to make my space mine each time we moved. It was all I had back then. We would break down a home and set up a new one in a weekend like a modern-day nomadic family."

Kelda hugged me. I felt small and vulnerable remembering this and watching Lu. I knew what she was doing in her pretty DIY room of this dingy house. In one corner was a record player. She was dancing to "Little Pink Houses" by John Cougar Mellencamp. But she wasn't just dancing. She had just come back from running and was now dancing and moving around to burn *extra* calories. Even though it was the middle of July, she had on thick sweats. Under the sweats, she had wrapped her thighs in Saran wrap to sweat even more. We watched as she finished exercising and lay down on her bed. She took her hands and wrapped them around her waist, trying to make her fingers touch. This would tell her how much more she had to lose in order for her fingers to touch around her waistline. After, she lay on her back and measured with her fingers how far out her hip bones were. Finally, she took her belly skin and rolled it in her fingers.

Kelda interrupted and asked, "Lu, why did you do that? Why roll the skin like that? I understand the other measurements you were taking, but what is that about?"

I took a deep breath and explained. "If you roll your skin and can feel the veins and capillaries, and it's a bumpy roll rather than a smooth roll, that is a result of having absolutely no subcutaneous fat. If it is smooth when you roll the skin, there is a layer of fat cushioning your veins and capillaries. I still do it sometimes."

"Oh, honey..." Kelda's voice trailed off as if she wasn't sure what more to say.

I shrugged. It must have been the afternoon because Lu's mom walked in wearing her nurse's uniform and said, "Hey, honey, I have to go to work now. Dinner is in the Crock-Pot. I love you, baby girl."

Sarcastically, Lu replied, "Okay, Mom." And under her breath, she said, "Like I'm going to eat that garbage." Lu knew she had a binge planned, including the cake and ice cream she had squirreled away in the freezer where her mom wouldn't find it.

"What?"

She said, "I love you too, Mom. Have fun at work. I'll see you in the morning."

"That's what I thought you said."

Lu then waited for her mom to drive away. She made sure no one else was home and then very quickly went to her closet. Inside her closet were two buckets full of the contents of her stomach from her last binge and purge. She very carefully and swiftly took them to the bathroom and dumped them down the toilet. The surface of the contents was shiny and thick. It was last night's dinner. The grease, mucus, and food remnants stuck to the side of the buckets as she dumped them into the toilet. We watched as she gagged a little bit from the smell of it. She then took them outside and hosed them off, dumping the contents into the bushes. She got a bunch of paper towels and wiped them dry and then carefully placed them into the back of her closet to patiently wait for her next binge and purge.

Kelda looked at me. I was crying. Kelda said, "Tell me what you're feeling now."

"It's just that I know that this was a part of my life, and I know that I did this. And I know the strength and rage it took to do it. I just haven't thought about it in so long. I remember the feeling of panic and chaos at feeling fat. And yet it's not even about the fat. It's not about that. It never was. It felt like I was living this uncontrollable life. Moving here and there. My mom's emotional outbursts and verbal assaults. The assaults that happened inside the relationship with my boyfriends that were dressed as love but felt horrible. The only thing I could do, the only thing that made sense to me, was to eat everything in my sight and then purge so it didn't stick to me.

"I ate to purge. And I threw up, and I threw up, and I threw up until I was empty. For me, weight loss had to do with control, but more importantly, how powerful it felt to be able to eat something and decide to reject it from my body. Bulimia became a metaphor for my life. *I can eat this and get rid of it. I can withstand this pain, and then I can get rid of it just as easily.* Just like that. I didn't even have to stick my finger down my throat; it just came up. It would pour out of me, and I would feel cleaned. I would feel purified. I would feel purged of all of the things in the day I had to smile and nod to. All of the transgressions I had to allow.

"Kelda, I struggle to see how going over this is important in understanding that I was doing it from a place of love. The reason I ask that is because you say, 'Nothing but love.' I don't get it. Help me find the love in this; I only see it coming from a place of self-hate. Help me understand. Why are we here? The other things that happened in my life, I can understand. I was a victim. They were pushed on me. These people did these things to me, and I was strong and persevered and got through them.

"But, Kelda, I did this to me. Why did I do this to me? Why was I trying to literally blow up the contents of my body every day, several times a day? The insanity that raced through my brain as I filled my heart and body with food. When would I binge next? What would I eat? Where would I do it? The secrecy and isolation and planning around how I would get it out without being caught. My days were filled with covering up my behavior. I was a junkie. Food was my heroin. After I purged, I would go into a fog. If I knew what heroin felt like, I would imagine that the post-purge numb and floating, self-hating fog is similar to it. *How* is this helpful?"

Kelda replied, "The experience of what you have gone through—that you did not choose heroin, that you chose a coping mechanism so interconnected with your body—is no mistake. Your journey is intricately wrapped up with your bulimia. With every purge, you cleared your body of the pain of the day. It was your way. Without it, you might have done something else, something more like heroin or another addiction. I'm not saying it was the right way. I would not recommend bulimia as a solution for anything. But it did start off as a way to help you feel in control of something. Anything. Because we're being honest here, your life up until this point was very hard. People hurt you. They took advantage of you. They abandoned you. And you, as a child, needed to feel in control of something. What else does a child have to control? Their grades? Their athletics? All of the things we could name come from the same place: a need to be perfect. And because you had no control, no other way, you controlled the one thing you could—the food you ate.

"Purging, like any other addiction, is not a solution. It's a means to an end. It's a chapter in your life because before you could accept the truth of all that happened, you needed to hide from it a bit longer. That was your way. I want you to know it's many people's ways. This is how we get to the place of surrender and eventually reach up for help. But we're not there yet. There's more to this story. And I want you to pay attention here. Lu doesn't need your pity. This isn't a 'poor Lu' moment; it's simply the truth of what happened so we can cleanse the past. Remember, water is the way."

Kelda and I were back at Sadie's, sitting at the kitchen table. Lu's light came on. It was time to fly back to her world. I heard the subtle swishing of water.

"It looks like Lu needs us again." Kelda took my hand in hers, and we flew from the light to the dark, back to the light, and right back into my history, Lu's world …

We entered the living room of the rented house where Lu, her mom, brother, and sister lived. My lungs felt tight, and it was difficult to breathe. We could hear Lu just outside the front door, fumbling in her backpack for her housekey. While I understood that energies aren't incredibly noticeable to the human eye, Kelda and I could see that when Lu opened the front door, a fog of dark energy wafted out the door from the inside of the house onto the porch. We watched as she entered and quietly closed the door behind her. There was a dark cloud of doom all over the house. It felt creepy, and I knew what was coming. Kelda reached out and took my hand and simply said, "Breathe." I took a deep breath.

It was afternoon, after school. It was a Thursday.

Lu coughed a little bit as she walked in. She sighed deeply, cleared her throat, and went to the kitchen. She was thinking, hoping, and praying that she could get a small binge and purge in before her mom woke up. She put her book bag on the dining table and walked to the fridge. She got out a box of cereal and some milk. Perfect for binging, and even more perfect for purging. Cereal had a satisfying crunch and sweetness. It was a full sensory experience. And then purging cereal was very easy as long as it went down with plenty of milk.

The phone rang. Lu answered it.

"Hello. Hey! Hi! Yeah, like wasn't today so totally funny? Like, I couldn't believe that Mr. Tanner didn't notice that his fly was down like the whole class! I, like, totally couldn't stop staring at his crotch! I was laughing so hard. Then he was like, what? And I looked down again, and he was like 'Oh shit!' and zipped up his fly. Like, I could have died for him—*so* embarrassing! What a nerd! Oh my God! It, like, totally made my day. Dude! Oh my God! So yeah, there's a rager at Christy's house tomorrow. Wanna go? Awesome! Okay, yeah, I'll tell my mom I'm staying at your house, and you can tell your mom you're staying at mine, and then we can, like, totally rage all night! Totally, yeah. Let me see if I can do that. I haven't talked to my mom yet today. I think she's still sleeping."

I said to Kelda, "Oh how I spoke way back in the early eighties. It was totally valley girl. Like, oh my God, it's almost comical! My mom worked nights as a nurse and would sleep until the afternoon. Sometimes I would get home before my brother and sister and check out what kind of mood Mom was in. I would meet my brother and sister at the door and say, 'Watch out. Mom's in a bad mood.' That usually meant that she was drunk and angry, usually because of something we did or because she was sick of her life and being a single mom. My mom worked hard for us. I don't pretend to say she didn't. But in all her hard work and in all of my dad's serious business about God and his church, no one ever taught us about happiness. No one taught us about feeling content or connecting through love instead of pain. It was very confusing growing up in that house. When my dad lived with us, they fought all the time. They were never happy and always frustrated about the lives they had been dealt. Sure, they would laugh about things, but their humor was always sarcastic and left you feeling a little cut by the jokes. Like the reality of their comments hit deep. Do you know what I mean?"

Kelda nodded as we turned back to listen to Lu's phone conversation.

"Yeah, okay, I'll call you back about tomorrow. Fer sher!" Laughing, she said, "Yeah, we should get some cloves and wine coolers and party in style! Like, I feel so cool smoking cloves. I love them. Whatever. Yeah, I know they're bad for you, but they make me buzzed—and guess what? No calories! Like, then I can just sip on one of those coolers and smoke cloves all night. Ha-ha, yeah, I guess it's getting to be my thing! Ha-ha yeah, like, whatever. Okay, cool. I'll call you back."

Lu tiptoed up to her mom's room to check on how she was and what kind of mood she was in. Sometimes her mom would open her eyes, smile sweetly, and say, "Hey, baby girl." Other times, she would just roll over and turn her back to Lu. On this day, Lu decided to take a quick glance at herself in the mirror of her mom's bathroom before she entered the bedroom. She felt kind of lightheaded and wanted to make sure she looked okay. Instead, she noticed a bunch of opened prescription bottles on the counter. The faucet was dripping, and there was a handful of little blue pills in the bottom of the sink, slowly dissolving from the dripping water. Lu immediately knew something was wrong. She grabbed her middle and held her breath as a sticky tar feeling erupted in her stomach. It tasted bitter in her mouth, and she physically shuddered as the doom engulfed her.

Kelda and I could see a dark energetic fog all around the room. It was at Lu's ankles and, like a cloud, rose up toward the light bulb hanging in front of the vanity. The fog came from her mother's bedroom. Lu reached for the handle and opened the door to look. Her mom looked asleep, but something wasn't right. There was another empty bottle by her bedside. Lu gasped, and her breathing became short, frantic breaths as she searched the room for answers.

Suddenly she was shouting, "Mom? Mom? *Mom*!"

Lu ran to the bed, but her mother didn't move. She shook her gently at first, but she wouldn't open her eyes. So she shook harder and tried to pry her eyes open. Her eyeballs rolled to the back of her head—no response. Lu bent down to see if she was breathing. She could feel a slight breath, just a shallow exhale, but it was there.

She touched her neck and felt her heartbeat. She was still in there. "Okay, fuck, shit—what do I do?" Lu said.

Then she screamed, "Mom!"

Nothing.

She paced around the room, trying to decide what to do.

Kelda said, "Nine-one-one." I looked at Kelda. What was she doing?

Kelda sensed my confusion and said, "Sometimes our role is to help. When we witness events like we are now, we can have a little effect on what's happening. I am planting the thought in Lu's mind about what to do. We can't make her do it, but we can inspire the thought that she can act on if she chooses to."

Almost instantly, Lu said, "Mom! I'm going to call 911! Mom, I'll be right back! Oh my God, Mom, don't die! Mom!" Lu ran to the kitchen and dialed 911. She gave the details and told the lady to send an ambulance quickly. She made sure the front door was open and then ran back to her mom's room. Lu held her mom's limp body in her arms. Her mom made a few moaning sounds.

"Don't die, Mom. Don't die, Mom. I love you, Mom. Please, I need you. Please don't die. Wake up! Wake up!"

Eventually, the paramedics arrived. They made her mom throw up, and the same little blue, half-dissolved pills streamed out of her body. They put an oxygen mask on her face and said they needed to pump the rest of her stomach at the hospital. They would keep her for observation. As they brought in a stretcher to transport her, Lu's sister arrived from school.

She ran into the house screaming, "Mom!" just as the paramedics were wheeling her out of her bedroom.

"Oh, Kelda, I remember this. My sister and I held each other for what felt like forever. It was just the two of us until our neighbor Judy came to check on us. She had seen the ambulance lights and wanted to see if we were okay. Judy was a friend of my mom, so we knew we couldn't tell her the truth. We knew Mom wouldn't want her to know the truth. Somehow that would be bad for Mom. So instead, I said, 'Mom wasn't feeling well. She ate something bad at work last night, and she's been sick all day. They took her in for some tests. That's all we know.'

"Judy left after five minutes. We never even invited her in. She told us to call her if we needed anything. I can promise you, we didn't. The only person besides Mom we wanted with us that day was Dad, and we had no way to reach him. So we cleaned up the house. Neither of us knew what to say. Three days would pass before we saw Mom again, and when she came home, she was mad. Really mad. Apparently, calling 911 and having her go to the hospital where she worked wasn't a good idea.

"When my mom's rage was directed at me, I always envisioned her opening the top of my head and the door to my heart and vomiting words of hate directly into me. After the trip to the hospital, she was really angry at me. I always thought it was because

I saved her life. She said I humiliated her by calling the ambulance. I didn't understand that. How could saving her life be the thing that enraged her the most? She told me over and over that I was wrong about her behavior. She just wanted to sleep; that's why she didn't take *all* the pills. Just enough to knock her out for a while. How was I supposed to know the difference? She was unconscious!

"But rage wasn't new to my mother. She yelled more than I could handle. I had a yelling corner that I went to when it was too much. Maybe there was a plant there. I can't remember. But I would go there when she got really mad, and she would follow me and yell and yell and yell. She would be in a blind rage, and I would roll up into a protective ball with my hands over my head. Anything to stop the yelling. I would rock back and forth as she hurled her pain and anger at me. Her eyes would bug out, and the veins in her neck would pulse. Back then, anything could set her off. She wasn't okay. She tried to act okay, but she wasn't. As a kid, I thought I should be the one to fix her anger. I was used to her rage. To me, it wasn't new. In fact, it felt ancient. Just like my reaction. I swear, Kelda, we've done this dance a million times over a million lifetimes.

"When she was really mad, I would binge more than normal. I would binge so that I could purge. It felt as if purging was my body letting go of the rage. Let me show you what I mean. There is this one time, Kelda, I have a hard time letting go of because it's so humiliating. And sad. Should I show you? I think it might be good for me."

"Yes, take me there. Tell me when."

"Thanksgiving when I was fifteen."

And off we went in the familiar sideways direction, like a movie on high speed.

We arrived at the same house. There was a big Butterball turkey on the table, full of stuffing; a green bean casserole with Campbell's cream of mushroom soup and crispy onions on top; sweet potatoes baked with sweetened condensed milk and topped with roasted mini marshmallows; and mashed potatoes and gravy. Julia really made everything happen when it mattered (or when people were watching). There was even cranberry jelly, straight from the can and sliced on a plate next to the Jell-O salad. For dessert, pumpkin pie, apple pie, fresh whipped cream, and ice cream. As we watched, we saw that Lu was not being very helpful preparing the meal. With her bulimia out of control, she was deep in her world of avoiding food. Lu depended on controlling this part of her life so that she felt in control of something. What she couldn't see was that it had full control of her now. We watched as she danced around the room, doing aerobics to work off the calories from the meal she was about to be forced to eat.

I said, "God, Kelda, Thanksgiving was a torture to me. I made myself scarce for every one of them that I could avoid, and this year was just the same. Seems no one was very helpful to Mom."

We watched as Julia worked alone in the kitchen and saw all she had accomplished on her own. Looking at her, she had changed a bit. She had a curly perm that fell over her forehead in tight ringlets. She also had her ever-present glass of wine and ice cubes in hand. We watched the family eat the meal in almost total silence. Shelly (Lu's sister) tried hard to compliment Julia on a delicious meal. Billy (Lu's brother) sat slumped in the chair and talked about the Popeye Adventure Hour Thanksgiving Special he had been watching a few minutes before. Julia sighed a lot and ate in silence. Lu's eyes looked vacant. She kept her head down and just ate. One plate after the next of food.

"The turkey is really good, Mom," Lu said, looking up with a forced smile. While for many people this is a normal occurrence at Thanksgiving, for Lu, it was a binge. A regular meal for Lu would have been a fraction of what she put on her plate as her first helping.

These were hard times for Julia. They were hard for everyone. The longer the meal went on, the more agitated Lu seemed to become.

I looked at Kelda and explained, "I knew I couldn't go to the bathroom to purge, so I was stuck trying to figure out how to get rid of all this food that was now causing me to feel uncomfortably anxious. I could feel the calories turning to fat, padding my boney figure with a fat suit of calories and lumpy imperfection."

Lu got up and said, "Mom, this was really delicious. I'll be right back. I forgot I told Lucy I'd bring her some pie." She grabbed a big slice of pie and headed to the door. Julia, Shelly, and Billy just sat there looking at one another.

Billy said, "Her loss. More pie and ice cream for me!"

Julia put down her fork, set her elbows on the table, and rested her head in her hands. She took a deep breath and said, "You're sure right, kiddo! More for all of us!"

Lu had to get rid of the food. She felt desperate to make that happen *now.* She left the house and rode her bike to the local elementary school down the street. She rode holding the handlebars with one hand, and with the other hand, she shoved the big slice of pie down. There were kids playing on the playground, and she was sweating and in a panic. This was a very California-style school, with all the hallways and walkways between the classrooms outside. She walked past the classrooms looking for a trash can. She couldn't find any trash cans private enough to not get caught or seen. With panic pulsing through her, she found a garbage dumpster toward the back of the school behind the library. It was perfect. Before jumping in the dumpster, she turned to a nearby water fountain and gulped down as much water as she could take in. She knew that the pie crust would be hard to get up without water. She jumped in, squatted down, and wretched into an empty box inside the dumpster. She threw up every last bit of food in her belly until it was puddled around the tips of her Reebok high-tops. First to come up was the pie, greasy turkey, green beans swimming in stuffing, and mashed potatoes. Ribbons of cranberry sauce and mucus ran together. Bile and stuffing, buttered bread rolls turned to wet clumps of dough and snot. It all came up. All the way to the very first thing she ate, which was a handful of Cheetos. The orange Cheeto color was used as a marker to let her know she was nearing empty in her stomach.

She was momentarily free of all the rage. All that was left was emptiness and numbness. Out of breath and feeling dizzy, a wave of relief washed over her.

She backed up and sat there a moment, catching her breath. She wiped her mouth on someone's old homework, wiped the vomit splashes off the front of her Reeboks, and climbed out of the dumpster unseen.

Lu smiled and straightened up, only to see a little kid looking at her quizzically, like, *What the heck? Did that girl just climb out of that dumpster?* She walked past him and started running. She grabbed her bike and raced home just in time to help with the dishes. No one really cared much that she had been gone. They were all sacked out on the sofa or the floor watching something on TV. Julia was asleep. Safe! Whether it was out of guilt or another way to wipe clean what she had just done, Lu did all the dishes and cleaned up the whole kitchen so that it would be nice and clean for Julia when she woke up. Instead of putting all the leftover food in the refrigerator, Lu split it up. She put some on paper plates stacked on top of each other and covered with paper towels in the garbage can. Then she put the rest in Tupperware and tucked it on the shelves in the refrigerator so that Julia would not think that she wasted any food. Once the kitchen was spotless with decoy leftovers in the fridge and her next binge secretly hidden in the garbage, she slumped on a bean bag next to her brother, who was lying on the floor. A slight smile of satisfaction on her face revealed the relief of getting away with it. She was back in control! She was back on top of her game. No fat suit today.

"Dang, Kelda, that was intense! Do you know I remember this and many other meals like it? On days when I actually ate a meal, I always added an extra hour or two to my exercise routine to make sure no fat globules formed on the inside of my skin. I would also take a laxative so that any of the food that was absorbed into my system was liquified and removed by my intestines later in the day. This was how I stayed in control. And as gross as it was and as crazy as it sounds now, it was all I had."

Kelda said, "My dear, offer yourself some grace. The memory is not quite over."

Much later that night, while everyone was asleep, we watched as Lu got up and tiptoed to the kitchen.

"Oh, Kelda! This is tough to watch. Such a seesaw of control and utter lack of control at a basic animal level."

We watched as Lu crept into the kitchen. She got down on her hands and knees and started digging through the garbage, looking for the plates of food she had put there earlier. She had a half-eaten turkey leg in one hand and cold mashed potatoes in the other. She ate pieces of pumpkin pie and stuffing right out of the garbage can. She washed it down with giant glasses of water. She was blind with hunger and rage and completely out of control. Just Lu. By herself in the middle of the night, eating from the garbage. To not wake anyone up, she only threw up in the toilet once. One flush meant someone had to pee in the middle of the night. But that wasn't enough to get everything out, so she snuck to the back of her closet and quietly got out the empty buckets.

She quietly went outside and once again emptied the contents of her stomach. Grateful for the sliding glass door in her room, Lu's easy access to privacy and silence allowed her to let go of everything without a soul knowing. When she purged, she released her inability to control her family. She purged her failure to heal her mom. She purged her hatred at not being pretty enough. Funny enough. Smart enough. Popular enough. Perfect enough. She purged it all. Then she cried. Silent tears of relief. When it ended, she lay on her back, looking up at the stars in the night sky, and floated away.

We heard her say to herself, "At least I have this. At least I had control over something."

"Funny thing, Kelda. The month before Thanksgiving, I was riding in the back of a convertible Thunderbird around the football field, waving at hundreds of people. I had been voted to the homecoming court. I didn't win, but it was something all high school girls dreamed about as the high point of their high school careers. Many people thought I was sitting in that car feeling really good about myself. How amazing to be driving around with a beautiful formal gown on, a tiara on my head, as other students clapped and cheered for me? Nope! I was consumed with panic that my family would discover the unemptied buckets of vomit in my closet from earlier that day. That's what I was thinking about. That hateful, eating-disordered brain ran wild inside me as I put on a plastic face and waved at my friends. All the while, I heard whispering in my ear, 'Look at you, the homecoming princess with buckets of vomit hiding in her closet. You're disgusting.'"

With those words lingering in the air, we returned to Sadie's to talk about what we had just witnessed. These talks were a very important part of the healing. So was being at Sadie's. Sadie's was a deeply healing place. There were many aspects to it. It spread out like a house, but it was more than that. We were back on the sofa. The ever-present serving of cookies and cocoa were nearby.

"Ugh. I can't do this anymore, Kelda. It's too much. It's too hard. I'm wrecked going back through all this stuff. Perhaps memories aren't supposed to be relived like this. It seems like there was a very good reason why I chose to forget these things. Thank God for that cup of forgetfulness. Remembering is brutal. Tell me again how this is going to help me, not just retraumatize me?"

"It is how you approach the trauma that determines the re-traumatization. This is why we looked at each trauma from the lens of love. Trust me, it's okay that you feel this way right now. Let the tears flow. Tears are okay. Water is the way after all."

"Okay."

"The intention of remembering isn't to hurt you; it is so that you reconnect with the truth, feel it, and then let it go. This transforms the stale feelings. It's almost like a chemical change. Before you feel it, the energy of the emotions are stuck in your very cells. Like sticky glue or old tar on a blacktop. When you feel it, it breathes new life into those stale, old parts so you can transform them. Those parts of you that have been stuck in memories for so long. Feeling it is what's required so you can release it. It has to be done in a safe place, but when you do this, you create the experience required to let it go. You can't truly let go until you do all three parts: remember, feel, and release.

"An example you can probably relate to is how your body transforms through exercise. Do you remember what it feels like when you first exercise after a hiatus and all of your muscles are sore?"

"Yeah, the other day after exercising, I could hardly walk up the stairs, my legs were so sore."

"You probably already know, but this type of muscle stiffness or achiness is normal. It doesn't last long and is actually a sign of your improving fitness. The soreness is due to little micro tears in your muscles from exerting them. Most people feel kind of good about sore muscles. It means they've had a good workout. That metaphor holds here too. As we go back and revisit your past, the feelings around them can be likened to this same pain. You are going back and lifting the heavy weight of the past. That experience is a hard emotional and mental workout. Metaphorically, it's creating tiny micro tears in your system. We need to treat the pain with comfort and gentleness, just as if your muscles were hurting.

"If you were to look at your pain and sorrow with the same approach as you do with your sore muscles, you may see things differently, instead of feeling, 'I would be better off not revisiting this pain' or 'it would be easier to skip this part.' Neither is really true. When someone is ready to release the pain of the past, the path is always the same: remember, feel, and release. That is the path to transformation. It builds your internal fortitude and creates an incredible sense of pride and trust in yourself. Because you did it. You faced it. You got honest and honored your true self, and there's nothing more powerful for transformation than the truth.

"From experiences like this, you learn that you get stronger. Your sense of self stabilizes and takes deeper roots than you've ever had before, because they are *your* roots, not those of your ancestors or the people who came into your life.

"No one can give you back the innocence that was taken from you. So, we won't pretend that this was 'good for you,' but you are to witness your life so you can understand the importance of it and love yourself from a place of pure love. You are not what happened to you. This experience is rewriting your internal system. Your very DNA will change though this transformation, and your stories and experiences will be seen through the lens of love and courage. Lu, you did not go through these things just to be a symbol of victimization. You are a way out of the darkness for others who have gone through similar or worse experiences. The reasons we are in these bodies are never—I repeat, *never*—arbitrary. As you transform the sticky glue of the past, you will become a voice and a vision for anyone else on their own version of this journey."

"But I don't always want to do this."

"Of course not. That's the beauty of doing it now. It will never be the 'first time' again. Forever more, when you remember, you will do it through eyes and a heart full of perspective. And I am with you always. You will never be alone. And you never have to go back to hating your body or your heart ever again.

"My dear, you have entered the final part of your transformation. This is the doorway to the beliefs you created yourself. Ones that you made true in the face of contrary evidence. Truths that, despite healthy people or positive circumstances, you ignored because of what you held to be true. And now it's time to dismantle those as well so you're free. That's my greatest wish for you. Will you join me?"

"Water is the way."

"Water is the way."

Searching for Pennies at the Bottom of the Well

She woke up feeling hungover and ashamed, again. Even though she was only nineteen, Lu had become very familiar with the feeling of shame. Lu moved out of her house when she was seventeen, but because of the amount of drugs and alcohol she was doing, she had lost her job. She flunked out of junior college and was falling apart. So with nowhere else to go, she moved back in with her mom while she got it together for a few months—just until she had enough money to move out again. Lu did this two or three more times throughout her young adult life. Each time, it was harder and harder to return home, until finally it became an unimaginable choice.

She stood in her room in her mom's house where everything was painted black. When she moved back in, she painted the whole room black, except for one wall and the ceiling. All the furniture was black. The dresser with little pink flowers on the handles, black. The desk her mom had splurged on so that she would have a better place to study for school, black. Her room had two twin beds from when she and her sister slept in them as bunk beds.

Sissy on the top bunk, Lu on the bottom. She used to have a Shaun Cassidy poster taped to the underside of the top bunk, and she would give him a kiss every night before she went to sleep. Shaun Cassidy protected Lu from the demons in her dreams and in her memory. The bunk beds, now un-bunked, were painted black.

Lu was good at sewing, so she sewed black and white checkered fabric over the top of her pink comforters. She made two bright red throw pillows for each bed and found an amazingly cool Nagle poster at the swap meet. It was from the eighties, with the sunglasses and red lipstick. Wilumina's darkness (with a splash of color) was complete. It expressed how she felt.

In contrast, she lived in a world full of color. She had been working in retail for a few years and sewing her own clothes. Fashion was everything to her. Her hair was permed, and she teased those permed curls into a mass of fluff. Especially the bangs. They were perched on the front of her head like some kind of lopsided sun visor. She cemented the fluffy, teased curls into place with a combination of Aussie Mega Babe hairspray and L'Oréal mousse. Her hair looked like a cemented "brillo pad" of hard, tangled, bright yellow, curly perfection. She would then paint rainbows on her eyelids with wet n wild eyeshadow. The bright shadow made perfect lines of rainbow colors from her lash line to her eyebrows. She was blessed with heavy, dark eyebrows like Brooke Shields's. And she wore the fashion to match. All of her outfits were full of color and the best shoulder pads she could find.

But at home, in the darkness of her mother's house, she felt the heaviness of her family, her history, and all of it lived inside her—as dark and black as her black, black room.

The closet of her room had floor-to-ceiling mirrored doors that Lu would stand in front of religiously, measuring her waistline.

She would wrap her hands around her waist to see how good she was. If her fingertips could touch like a super tight finger belt, then Lu was doing "good." She would smile and look at herself, swaying back and forth to get a better look at the tiny profile of her waist.

She would think, full of pride, *How many other people have a waist this small?* Then she would wrap her fingers around her wrist and see how far she could pull them up her arm without breaking the contact of her forefinger and her thumb. If she could get them up to her elbow without breaking, she was thin enough. Then came the final measurement; if she could roll the skin on her belly and still feel the veins and capillaries as bumpy, then she was thin enough.

If that feeling of rolling the skin on her belly ever felt smooth, that meant that she had too much subcutaneous fat, and she would have to adjust her eating and exercise routine. On days when she felt the fat under her fingers, she would double her effort to lose that fat. No fat was allowed. She exercised and worked out obsessively, which meant she had some muscle in her legs, but no fat was allowed on her tiny waistline or on her arms.

Those were Lu's comfort zones. Her waist and her arms kept her feeling safe and capable. The world could be falling apart all around her, but if her belly had no fat that she could feel, she was okay. She was safe.

When Kelda and I dropped in, Lu was having a hard time controlling her bulimia. She was binging and purging more than usual. She was losing control. The thing with binging and purging is that no matter how hard you try to get rid of the food when you binge, some of those calories stick. Lu was gaining weight. She thought that some of the weight was from the times when she binged and, for whatever reason, was interrupted or prevented from fully purging. This would cause her a penetrating feeling of being out of control. The massive anxiety attack that followed was from the guilt and the awareness that she was getting fat. There were nights when she would lie in bed sure that she could feel the fat molecules expanding in her body.

She was filled with shame. No matter what she did, she could not control her weight or the need to binge and purge. All of this grew from her deep knowing that she was not really in control of anything in her world. If people could abuse her, violate her, and rob her of her dignity as they had without penalty, then certainly she was not in control of anything.

The first few years after her mom's suicide attempt, Julia spent a lot of the time in her bed. Gone were her mom's manic Copacabana days of dancing and twirling around the living room. Julia was in a long sad, depressive state. She got up and went to work, made dinner, and paid the bills. But she stopped cleaning and taking care of herself and was incapable of being there for Lu or her siblings. Julia's pain consumed her, and it left her blind to her children's pain. The signs and signals that her kids were not doing well were lost on Julia. Lu knew her mom was suffering, but she didn't see any way to help her. Every now and then, Lu wished she could speak to her dad about her mom's sadness. Get advice for what to do. But then she remembered that he was not there. This, too, made her feel out of control. Who do you turn to when your parents are not capable of caring for you?

Lu discovered cocaine in high school. It was like a miracle for her brain. Having undiagnosed ADHD, it felt like her brain thrived on cocaine. It came alive—an experience that no amount of caffeine could duplicate. Lu didn't drink much in high school because of the calories, but she would smoke cloves, because they made her feel lightheaded. But as she got older, the value of the buzz from alcohol outweighed the calories. By nineteen, Lu drank her dinners instead of eating her food.

Because of her low weight, when she drank, she almost always got very drunk. She would black out and not remember much of what happened. But once she discovered that a little bit of cocaine would allow her to drink more and not pass out or black out, cocaine and alcohol became her go-to evening meal. Then cocaine became a part of her breakfast and lunch. It was one of her favorite food groups. She found it went well with everything she did. And the more she partied, the more opportunities showed up for crack and other harder drugs. Just before she fully stepped into that world, she said no. The lure of harder drugs both scared her and allured her.

Her feelings of being out of control were taking over. Her old measurement systems were still firmly in place, but because of the alcohol, binging, and purging, her body was bloated, and her mind felt very unstable. When she reached her fingers around her waist, they wouldn't touch all the way, and she felt panic. It was at this moment that she first thought that she'd rather die than be fat. She heard in her mind the words "Do it!" In that moment, in her black room, death felt like an option. The hope she had been holding onto was fraying. In its place were hangovers and shame. Out of the corner of her eye, she saw a black shape pass behind her.

Panicked, she said, "Who's there?"

But there was no response.

"Kelda?" I said.

"Yes, my love…"

"Who—what was that?"

"What do you think?"

"I don't know! I just know it scares me."

We turned back to see Lu start to move slowly, swaying in the mirror. The black shape was darkness. It was evil. It was cold, and it was calculating. It looked as if it was propositioning Lu. Like it was waiting to be given a chance. Suddenly, it looked as if Lu was losing grip; if she didn't hold on, it was going to take her down the path of destruction.

We could see confusion on her face, but she just continued to stare into the mirror in a trance. She turned and watched as it wrapped itself around her. It twirled her around, touching her and delighting in her confusion. The darkness was drawing her in, tempting her with promises to end her pain and confusion. It was sadistically courting her, saying, "Drink me in. Dance me into your heart. Let me take away your pain. Come! Come! You can always choose me, over and over again. You've come so close many times, but you've never succumbed to my desire, and yet I have been your constant partner. I have danced with you in your pain and your grief. Your misery and your confusion. All you need to do is make the choice, and all will get easier; all will be well."

We could see on her face that she felt tempted. She was drawn into the sense of safety being promised; of not having to try anymore; of being free from everything she tried so hard to control and escape that never, ever worked. Lu looked as if she were in a trance, lulled into a false promise that this would make everything easier. Tears streamed down her face, but the look she made mirrored joy. She was on the edge of surrendering to the darkness.

"I remember this moment," I told Kelda. "For a few seconds, I actually thought I could do it. I thought about hanging myself with the scarves in my closet or a bedsheet. I thought about slitting my wrists, but the blood was more than I could bear. I thought about taking pills like my mom. And that thought made sense."

We watched as Lu walked down the hall to her mother's bathroom. In her cabinet were loads of different kinds of pills. Lu found a few bottles that had a warning on the labels that said, "May induce drowsiness" or "Do not take while driving or operating heavy equipment."

We heard her say aloud, "Perfect. I want to leave this place."

The drugs in the bottles had long names ending in *pam*, *dal*, or *diene*. Many of the bottles were still partially full. Because her mom was a nurse, she always had a pill for everything that ailed anyone.

Lu said aloud, "My life is ailing me. Glad you have a pill for that."

We watched as Lu took a handful of pills from each bottle, mixed them all together, put them in the back pockets of her Levi 501s, and ran back to her room.

Back in her bedroom, Lu looked at herself in the mirror and said, "I'm not like her. She didn't do it all the way. If I do it, I'll finish the job.

"I could stop eating again and slowly waste away to dust."

Kelda and I both knew the other option was to call that guy Roy and get an overdose of cocaine.

Sitting with Kelda, watching Lu struggle with the decision to take her life, I asked, "How come I didn't do it? What kept me from giving in?"

"I suppose it comes down to who you really are on the inside. All your life, you have battled and danced with the darkness. Darkness in you and darkness around you. But there is also a tremendous light. Light that shines into the deepest crevices to let in one very special thing, hope. And that is what brought you through the well to me."

We turned to see Lu looking into the mirror. She dug all the pills out of her pants pocket and looked at them in her hands. She was crying, and we could hear her thoughts

What would life be like for everyone else if I'm not here?

Would they notice? Would they care? My mom swallowed pills. She opened the door to the possibility of leaving this world. If she could, why can't I?

Lu emanated deep pain and overwhelm. Life had always been so hard.

Then we heard another voice say, "Do it, Lu. Do it. No one would even notice."

Lu's thoughts responded, *Who was that voice? Is it me? Was it inside my head?*

She stared at the pills in her hands. Her hands were turning colors with the coating of the pills mixing with the sweat of her hands.

Her inner monologue continued. *If I'm going to do it, I better do it soon.*

Do I have enough? Should I get more?

Some were falling on the floor, so she put a few in her mouth and swallowed. She kept staring at the mirror. She looked like she was on the verge of passing out but then would come back to, blinking her eyes and staring at herself in the mirror. Her head rolled back and forth, and then she would intently focus back on her image in the mirror. Full of hate and resignation. She buckled to her knees. The pills fell all over the floor, leaving colorful stains on her hands like animal cookie icing.

I looked wild-eyed at Kelda and said, "This was such a confusing moment. Because in one breath, I wanted to die. And in another, there was a spark inside me that wanted to live. I need to tell her to live! Kelda, I can't let her die. I have to tell her to *live*."

I started shouting, "Wilumina, you need help! You don't need more hate. You need love!"

And Lu turned as if she heard a voice.

"Get help!" I yelled through time and space, sending all the love I had toward Wilumina's heart.

And at that moment, Lu seemed to straighten up a little. She looked up and took a deep breath and wiped her eyes. She looked straight at herself in the mirror and said, "No dying today. I want to live."

Her tone changed in an instant, and she seemed to be talking to herself. "You need some serious help, and you're in deep trouble, and no one is going to help you but you." She rushed to her toilet and threw up the few pills she had taken, then she lay on her bathroom floor next to the toilet.

I turned to Kelda. "She heard me! She heard me! I heard me!"

I turned back to Lu and shouted, "Yes, Wilumina, you are going to live! You are going to have so many adventures. You are going to travel all over the world. Give birth to two beautiful children. You are going to find love like you've never imagined! You are going to learn to help so many people. You have *so* much to give the world. You matter! I need you; the world needs you! You are going to write and love and live! God blessed, you are going to live!"

Kelda and I were hugging and laughing and crying as the vision faded from view. I caught my breath, and Kelda said calmly and firmly, "Let's leave Lu where she is for the moment. She's going to need to sleep those pills off, but she will be fine. Let's go back to Sadie's house and have a nice cup of cocoa and talk about it. Shall we? We both know that right after this, the very next day in fact, Lu found a therapist."

"Yes, exactly! I remember. It was a bulletin I saw on a poster board. The kind with the tear-off phone numbers on the bottom. It said in big letters, 'Do you have Bulimia? Are you between the ages of 18 and 21? Take part in a clinical trial for an experimental new treatment drug.' I tore off the number and called when I got home. I made an appointment the next day to enter the study, but I didn't actually do the study. I met Faith. Faith was a social worker, and she took me into her care, and that was what started my healing journey."

So we left Lu there on the bathroom floor, knowing that she was definitely not going to die. Lu was going to change course and begin the long, arduous process toward self-love and healing from trauma.

Into the Light

Kelda took my hand in hers as we faced each other, and we both said, "Nothing but love." We were transported back to Sadie's porch. The now familiar sound of buzzing that had terrified me at first gave me great comfort because I knew where it was taking me. Back to our little spot on Sadie's couch to talk.

As we made ourselves comfortable, I noticed that Kelda had something more in mind other than just another chat; I could see it in her eyes. They were loving and kind, but they sparkled with a mischievous knowing that I deeply wanted to know more about. Kelda smiled, patted my knee, and said, "All right then. Come with me."

We got up and went inside the house to the hallway of doors. I knew what this meant. I could see the second door on the left was glowing just a little bit. Kelda smiled and nodded her head as I began to walk toward the door. Kelda walked right next to me. She reached for my hand, and together we stepped over the threshold. I said, "Kelda, what's happening?"

"I am coming with you today."

Inside the door, Kelda began to lead me through a beautiful forest. It was shady and secluded, yet sunny and warm. There were bees buzzing and birds singing. The air smelled like pine moss and wildflowers. We walked down a little path, listening to a bird's song and the crunch of rocks beneath our feet. We walked through a little grove of trees to a clearing. Spread out in front of us were blankets and pillows. Next to them were two hollows dug into the earth. It was a peculiar site. I didn't know what the hollows were for, but I trusted Kelda. She walked forward and sat down on the blankets. I sat next to her, feeling the sun on my shoulders and face. There was a cool breeze that invited me to take a deep breath in. As we got comfortable, Kelda turned and looked at me and began speaking.

"We didn't go through all these experiences, my dear, for you to feel sad, victimized,

ashamed, guilty, outraged, or any of those emotions. Certainly, you have felt them. But those emotions aren't meant to take up a permanent place in your heart. Those emotions are meant to be moved through."

"We have definitely gone through them!" I agreed.

She continued, "Yes, we went through all these so that you could finally feel what it's like to be at peace in your body, at peace in your heart, at peace in your soul, and even at peace remembering the past. Do you remember way back when you drank from the cup of forgetfulness? It was so important to do that as a child. I don't believe you would have made it through if you had to remember every single detail of what happened to you. But now you need to fully remember. Today I'm going to give you another cup to drink from."

Kelda sat up straight and snapped her fingers three times. She raised her hand in the air, and as she did, the sky immediately above her hand started swirling like a cloud of dust and smoke, with sparkles of light and glitter dancing all around. The cloud rolled and twisted like a storm, and then as quickly as it started, it calmed down. A shape began to form in her hand. It was a cup. An earthenware cup. She placed it in front of me like a gift and motioned for me to pick it up.

Holding it in my hands, I felt uneasy. I looked at her and said, "Hold on. I'm scared."

She explained, "I understand. It can be very scary to let go of the forgetting. It's hard to let go of the spaces inside that hold all the memories the cup of forgetfulness took from you, all those spaces where the spiders live and feast on your pain and trauma. I know. It's hard to let go of the safety of what you think you know. The cup gave you a version of the world that you learned to live within. Without knowing what really happened, you still adapted to everything around you. Even when your life has been hard, certain feelings, thoughts, and behaviors are oddly familiar. Even without the complete truth, you created paths around your pain that allowed you to manage the all too familiar rage and fear. The feelings you experience are familiar territory for your brain and your body. You might even ask the question 'If I'm not this, then who am I?'

"But this is an incomplete version of who you really are. It is time to remember who you are. So that's what we're going to do now. But before you do, let me tell you a little bit about this cup of remembering, sweetie. It's going to make you sick. It might even hurt. Parts may feel scary and painful. Other parts will leave you feeling invigorated and alive. And when it's finished, this journey back to yourself, to your whole self, you will feel a love you've never experienced before. That is how this entire process becomes complete. It will leave you feeling a love for yourself you've never fully known before. That is my one true wish for you."

I looked her in the eyes, with the open heart of a child, and said, "Okay, Kelda. I trust you. I know with all my heart that you would not hurt me. You will not lead me astray. I know that completely. And looking back at all the things that we've gone through together, I also know how strong I am. I will offer that love and grace to myself as we go through this next part, whatever that is. The way I lived in the past was the only way I knew how to be. It was the only way I knew how to survive. I didn't know love for myself. I only knew sorrow and the desperate need to escape all that pain. I also know it was the path of my mother's life and of the women who came before me. But it's not supposed to be my life, is it, Kelda?"

Kelda quietly shook her head in agreement.

"Before I drink from this cup, I have a question. If I get rid of this old way of being, get rid of the pain and the grief that defined me for so long, what will I do then? My story is how I have connected to every person who's been close to me. Without it, who am I? How will I have any friends? How will I relate to anyone? Why would they want to be close to me if I'm not this person?"

Kelda responded, "I hope you're starting to see that the path ahead of you is not one where you connect with people through pain, but through the lens of love. That is the path ahead of you."

Looking down at the cup, I said, "You say that this will make me sick?"

"Yes."

"Okay, but this is a different kind of sick than my eating disorder, right?"

"Yes, this is a different sick. This sickness, the nausea you will feel, will be entirely different. In ancient cultures, purging is an important part of ceremonies and healing. This experience will help you tap into a strength that lies deep inside. It's older than you, wiser than you. It's based in ancient wisdom and comes from ancestral strength that lives deep inside your bones. It is different from your eating disorder. Nothing like it in fact.

"But I want you to think about something. What if your bulimia was just a way you chose to stay alive? With bulimia, you found a way to scream into the toilet all the things you couldn't say. That sickness came from a place of avoidance, fear, and self-loathing. This is different; this comes from life and from love.

"As you drink, taste the bitterness and the sweetness. Taste how both live on your tongue and in the back of your throat. Notice how the muscles in your throat want to constrict, but don't give in. Just breathe and swallow. Trust. Trust, my dear."

I looked down at the cup and with a trusting heart raised the cup to my lips. I swallowed the entire contents at once. I tasted the bitter and the sweet colliding in my mouth. My throat con-stricted, and I had an involuntary desire to push back what was about to happen. Then, choosing to not fight it, I lay back on the soft pillows. A slight euphoria came over me when I said, "Okay, I'm doing this. It's nice."

She said, "Yes, it is. Just breathe, my dear."

I breathed slowly and closed my eyes.

For moments, we were silent.

Then bright colors emerged in my mind. It was like watching a movie of random images, sounds, and sensations. They came quickly, and it changed from the joy of seeing colors and sounds to patterns that were confusing and a little scary. I heard music playing and opened my eyes to see Kelda playing a drum. She was humming a deep, soulful tune and swaying to the music. She looked at me and told me to trust the process. "Your brain is sorting through things right now, and you're simply witnessing it as the clutter is cleared out of your psyche."

I felt dizzy, so I closed my eyes and went back to the images. The images slowly started to shift from bright colors and geometric patterns to something a little more sinister.

I felt sick.

Images of what seemed like my childhood danced in front of me. As they came at me, the struggles I had with my mother came forward. The alley, Frank's face, my dad leaving, the time I struck a girl with a rock, other kids laughing at me, my mom yelling at me. It seemed like the memories and images were surrounding me. As they continued, I sobbed.

Kelda said, "Breathe," as she sped up her drumming. I felt another wave of nausea. It was accompanied by a feeling of warmth and tingling in my body.

I heard Kelda say, "Let it all simply pass through you. Breathe. Remember, nothing today can hurt you. Look at all the things you have survived."

I started shaking. The shaking scared me.

Kelda said, "Good, good. Let it out! Don't fight your body's need to shake." It wasn't like a seizure. It was like being super cold with strong shivers. Breathing, I witnessed images and faces and experiences from my life. Like a hall of mirrors, they passed by me. I curled into a ball. Then I straightened out and lay panting. The surge of images and feelings died down.

I began to wretch. I felt an arm around me. Kelda moved me to one of the holes dug in the ground. I heard her say, "Get on your hands and knees."

Following her instructions, I placed one hand on either side of the dirt hollow. She came over and put her hands over mine, "Feel the earth with your hands."

I felt the earth. Crying, I grabbed the dirt and felt the solidity of the earth in my hands and under my nails. It was cool and soothing.

Another wave of nausea came. Kelda said, "Yes! Let it come."

What I thought was going to be vomit came out as a scream. I screamed into the earth. I screamed everything I wasn't allowed to scream before. My eyes and nose were pouring with tears, mixed with a scream that came from deep in my soul. It came from some ancient memory, and I was screaming it back into the earth.

Then the images began again. I plunged deep down into what felt like hell. Then the images became almost black and white. I was running down a road of some sort. Where was I going? All around me were arms and legs coming up from the earth. I could hear moaning and groaning and people calling for me. Terrible, bloodied faces screaming as they raced past me. I was running and screaming. It was violent, and I was terrified.

I could hear Kelda in the distance saying, "Nothing here will harm you. Don't resist. Allow. Thank the pain. Thank the fear. Let it grow inside you. Let it grow in your mind. Let it become almost impossible. Yes, that's it! Make a noise, Lu! Lift your voice to this terror you are feeling! It is okay to scream now!"

As I screamed and screamed, Kelda reminded me to place my hands on either side of the hollow and let it go.

"Feel the earth! Be one with it. Connect to the earth!" she continued. "Mother Earth will support you. Let it out!" As I remembered vision after vision, experience after experience, I screamed it out. The visions transformed as the screams died down. With every image, every feeling that came up, I screamed until everything inside of me was emptied. I screamed until I had nothing left. It felt like a continuation of the experience I had when I first came to the well. Yet it was transforming. The screams changed. What felt like rage and fear in the beginning started to transform. There was power inside the scream, a voice that wasn't afraid but was in control. I felt strong and capable, not victimized or needy. Suddenly, I felt the urge to sit up and look around. Then instantly exhausted. I lay back down on my side and let out a great sigh.

Kelda said in her sternest voice yet, "Get up. Get up. Wilumina, get up now. Lift your head up. Straighten your spine."

I said, "But I'm tired."

She said, "Yes, I'm sure you are, and still you will lift your head. You will straighten your spine, and you will sit up."

I did as I was told and sat up with my spine straight and my eyes closed. Colors started to appear again.

But Kelda wasn't about to let me fall back into that state. Sternly she said, "Now, sit up with love. Let love be the strength in your spine."

I opened one eye and looked at her a little sideways. I smiled a half smile and straightened myself just a little bit more. I took a deep breath in and out. I was ready to listen.

She said, "You will continue to walk through darkness, and you will carry some of it with you everywhere. That is the experience of being human. From this day forward, you will experience it without letting fear make you cower or falter. Because you are capable of being fully present with your pain. You do not need to deny it ever again. In fact, you will not deny it. You will meet your darkness and your pain with love because those are the parts of you that need your loving kindness the most.

"That is your way forward, Lu. You have done well. You have faced your fears and your trauma. You have seen all of it, and you have witnessed the pain of a child and grown the compassion of an adult. You should be proud of yourself."

I beamed with her praise. Hearing her words made the journey feel complete. But Kelda in her infinite wisdom had one more gift to share.

"Would you like to see another aspect of yourself? I would like to show you who you really are," she said.

I said, "Okay," sitting up even more straight, with my head up.

Kelda said, "Good. Now close your eyes and breathe in through your nose, and as you exhale, sigh it out."

I did as she instructed.

Then Kelda snapped her fingers three times. With my eyes still closed, I could hear her start to hum as she began to play her instrument.

In my mind's eye, everything around me became white. I felt as if I was going up, up, up, like riding a roller coaster to the top— click, click, click. As we climbed, I could feel the wind. It started blowing faster and faster. It blew through my hair and then somehow transformed into laughter. I heard people shouting, "Hooray! We're so glad you're here!"

"Congratulations!"

"Look at you!"

"You should be so proud."

"Good for you! You did it!"

"Way to go!"

The messages kept coming from all around.

As my mind adjusted to what looked like a big castle or hall, the vast brightness began to come into focus. The movement around me began to slow down, and I could make out the image of what looked like angels or people in white robes. They were standing at a table.

"Hello," I said. Amazingly, I wasn't scared at all. I felt like I was speaking to friends, people who knew me, but I couldn't place how. It was a peace unlike anything I had ever experienced, and yet something about it was utterly familiar.

"Hello, Wilumina! We're overjoyed that you are here. It's not too often that we get to spend time with people. It would be our honor to show you something about yourself that you may have forgotten. It won't take but a moment, but I want to ask your permission first because once we show you, you will never be able to forget it. It's that important. Would that be okay with you?"

"Oh yes! I'm so honored to meet you too. Please show me."

The being farthest on the left walked over and started to pull back a curtain.

Someone said, "Come closer, my dear. Come closer." I walked right up to the curtain, not knowing if someone was behind it or if I was about to look into a magic mirror. Maybe it was who I would become after this journey with Kelda. The real Wilumina Florida Pearl. At first, it was just like looking into a mirror, but as they continued to pull the curtain back, all I could see was gold, shimmering sparkles. There wasn't any human form in front of me, even though it was clear I was looking into a mirror. Simply gold and light shining back at me.

I asked them, "What am I looking at?"

Together, they said, "You."

Someone else added, "This is who you really are. You're not the form you see in a regular mirror. Your true self is this. All this powerful, beautiful, illuminated light. This is who you are."

"This is who I am." As their words landed, my heart swelled, overflowing with love, and in that one precious moment, I fell in love. It was the most beautiful thing I'd ever seen. *I was the most beautiful thing I'd ever seen.*

Me. It was my soul. My spirit, my essence. It was what I came from and what I knew I would return to when my time on earth is done. As I witnessed the light, it called to me. I had an overwhelming desire to merge with the light. To go home to my real self.

Then someone said, "Not yet, dear. You're not quite ready."

"What? No!"

"You must return. Return to your life, your children, your family. You need to go back."

"But why?" I asked.

"Oh, my dear, your family and your girls need you. They need this new version of you more than ever. Especially now that you have seen your divine self. You see, Lu, humans have made a mess of the place. Not every soul looks like yours. Each soul has its own unique imprint that brings its own form of love and light to the planet. You see how beautiful you are?"

"So beautiful," I said in a daze. I was filled with such a desire to never go back. I wanted to stay in this love. "Please don't make me go back."

They said, "If only it was that easy. But on your journey, it's time to return to your life. Tell your story. Finish changing the story so your girls and their families keep changing the trajectory of trauma. It is time to speak your truth and use your voice. You get to return and live anew, with the wisdom from the cup of forgetfulness and the cup of remembering. We want you to show the people in your life that even though life on earth is hard and even though people are deeply wounded, the answer is love. Nothing but love.

"Finding your way back to your real self, your true essence, and feeling the love within you is your purpose, and we want you to share this love and all your knowledge with the world. The truth is the world needs you. They need your light to help shepherd people out of darkness. You are needed there. You're not needed here.

"Kelda wasn't just blowing glitter up your skirts when she said it. There is nothing but love! So now it's time to go home and be with your girls. And just know that we'll be here when you're ready to visit us again. Be brave, dear one, and share your wisdom with everyone you meet. And remember the power of your fierce voice and the deep power of love."

While those words were still lingering in the air, I was somehow back in the forest. As I blinked my eyes open, I realized I was lying in a different hollowed-out space in the earth. I must have moved during my soul connection moments. As I took in all that had happened, I lay there feeling held by the earth, safe and supported.

Kelda spoke quietly. "The earth is your mother. Let her hold you. She has the power to transform all the pain you shared and turn it into something beautiful. In the same way compost becomes fertilizer, Mother Earth will alchemize the pain you screamed at her and turn it into golden love. You see evidence of the alchemic process whenever you see a flower growing in a seemingly impossible place. Like a crack in a sidewalk or on the side of a cliff. Human mothers are flawed and unprepared. Mother Earth is flawless."

"I've got to tell you, Kelda, I've never felt more loved than I do right now. It's just me in the dirt, feeling all the love!"

Kelda and I both laughed, and as the giggles passed, a huge smile came across my face. "I really am nothing but love! That's what's inside there," I said, pointing to my body.

"Ahh, yes! If you unzipped your human form, you'd be nothing but stardust."

My eyes got really big, and I lifted my shirt, pretending to look inside, "Wow! No way! Stardust!" Then, as the joking subsided, I said, "But honestly, Kelda, I get it! I finally understand who or what I am. I *am* nothing but love. I always have been, and I always will be."

"Yes, you are! Now I'm not saying that you must be perfect or some kind of saint or anything. You're still very human, very flawed."

"Hey, easy there," I said, laughing and pretending to be offended.

Our joking was interrupted by a parade of tiny spiders. They were crawling out of the hollow in the ground that I had screamed into earlier. The light from above glistened off the shape of their tiny bodies. I watched in awe as dozens of them scurried over my foot. It tickled as their little legs marched over my skin. I didn't even think to move it out of their way.

We watched as the spiders scattered back into the shadows of the distant landscape, out of the light and back into the darkness. A few scurried in a different direction and up a nearby tree. They momentarily filled the tree with darkness. Through the darkness, I could see little bursts of light and then a flutter. Another burst of light and a flutter. The spiders were transforming. They were bursting into light and taking flight. The sound of flapping wings, feathers, and then a bird's song filled the space. Above us, a flock of white birds appeared, all singing in unison as they took flight and eventually disappeared from sight.

Kelda and I made our way back to Sadie's, where we placed an order for cocoa and a little plate of animal cookies. We sat in silence for a while, just breathing the love that we were feeling. Then I turned to Kelda. "So, from this time forward, it's not like I'm going to be miraculously, perfectly happy or healed all the way, right?"

Kelda laughed. "No, of course not. This isn't a fairy tale. This is life. Healing takes years. In some cases, it happens in an instant. But more often, it takes many, many instances over and over again."

I sat with that for a minute or two and then said in agreement, "It's an evolution. A back-and-forth learning spiral. Some days, all seems well, and then, well, then it's shit again."

She laughed at that. "Yes," Kelda said with a twinkle in her eye.

I said, "I know we've done a lot of work, but do we have to go through and heal all the traumas that I've had? Like each and every one? I've had so many. I've made so many mistakes. I was so hard on myself for so long. This healing thing seems impossible if we must look at every single one; we'll be here forever! I'm fifty years old, and we've barely covered the start of my twenties. Believe me, this was a big moment, but I was a total shitshow for a long time. Even though I found a better way, I still took a lot of detours before I gave up the self-loathing and self-harm."

Kelda smiled and said, "The experiences we have visited, these were your core wounds, the ones that shaped you—the ones that pulled the strings on all the other wounds, including all the wounding you did to yourself and to others. These experiences are directly and indirectly related to all the other things in your life."

"What about my mom, Kelda? She never forgave herself or others. In her life, she never got to release herself from the pain."

Kelda said, "For today, Lu, let's stay focused on your story. Your mother's life is her own story to unfold. Like yours, there are many layers. Many more than we will visit today. What I know for sure is that she has been the one to open your heart up to the master lesson you have been working on all this time. And that's the lesson on forgiveness."

Kelda went on, "Forgiveness is a tricky lesson to learn. It has two sides: the wound and the healing. To master forgiveness, there must be a wound, an incident or some pain that happens. From there lies the opportunity to forgive. One can't really happen without the other. No one learns forgiveness in the mind. So, it seems to me that your mom's part in your story is ultimately to teach you about forgiveness. The challenge now is that you also have compassion. Knowing what happened to your mom changes the story, right? You don't see her the same way you did even a few hours ago. So she's not the real person in the story to teach you about forgiveness. You are.

"To truly master forgiveness, Lu, you must learn how to forgive yourself. Do you understand what I mean?"

"Yes, I think so," I said, looking up and away as if searching for the words to my thoughts in the clouds. "Forgiveness of others is hollow, perhaps even impossible really, without first learning to love yourself and feel compassion for your own circumstances.

With those two things on board, it's easier to forgive others because your heart is clean. You're not doing to others what you wish someone would do for you. You're loving yourself and setting the stage for how you want others to love you."

"Yes, Lu. Your path to forgiving your mother, or anyone for that matter, is a road paved directly through your own heart."

Kelda smiled and scooted closer to me. "Come, let me hold you."

I slid next to Kelda and put my head on her shoulder as she moved to put both arms around me. She held me lovingly for a long time.

At some point, she started humming "Somewhere over the Rainbow."

I turned and looked at her and said, "That's my favorite song."

She just smiled and said, "I know."

Together, we sang softly, "Somewhere over the rainbow, way up high, there's a land that I long for, once in a lullaby."

I heard Kelda's voice come in clear, bringing me back to the moment, feeling her gently swaying as she caressed my temple.

"Lu, it's time for you to go back home."

"How will I ever thank you, Kelda?"

"Well, you can thank me by being different. Thank me by living differently. Now that you've opened this pathway, the door will never close. I'll see you again. But this, this was the big one. This experience will change your life and the lives of everyone you love and care about. You've heard people say that the chain of trauma was broken. This is that moment for you. You have broken the history of your family. Your girls and everyone who comes after them will never feel the pain and anguish you experienced. The link in the chain has broken. Now it's your job to create a new legacy for yourself and your future generations."

I was suddenly so incredibly tired. The moment was ending. It was sad and invigorating at the same time. The last thing I saw was Kelda's smile. She closed her eyes and touched my hands. I looked down and heard her say, "Water is the way."

And I replied, "Nothing but *love*…"

Far off in the distance, I felt a tug in my heart. Little Lu was saying something as my eyes floated closed and my journey back through the heavens, through the underworld, commenced.

I heard little Lu say, "Sometimes when I am sad for the little birdie that died but then flew away, I look up to the setting sun in the sky and think about it. Do you know how all the rays of light bounce off of the sun and make it look like elevators of light are surging up to the sky? I think that's the superhighway of souls coming and going from earth. I think that my birdie could be one of those souls. I think of that, and it makes me happy. Just like my middle name makes my mom happy. Seeing those rays of light makes me know that the souls have completed their work and they're jumping back into the light and traveling back to their homes in the stars."

Little Lu gave me one final way to remember that this was all very, very real. I felt myself jump onto one of those rays of light and headed back to my life and my mother's funeral.

The Awakening

I woke up in the courtyard next to the fountain. Both of my daughters were calling me.

"Momma? There you are!"

"Mom, we've been looking all over for you! You've been gone forever."

"Oh, I'm sorry, girls, I must have fallen asleep."

I thought, *How funny. Luckily, this place is so big. I wonder if anyone saw me.* I had fallen asleep on a little patch of grass next to the water fountain. That's when I noticed I was covered with a blanket. Someone must have seen me and gave me a blanket but did not wake me. The kindness in that random act touched me, and I started to cry.

"Don't cry, Mama," they both said.

"No, I'm okay. These are happy tears. I'm happy, sweet girls, so happy."

Just as I was getting up, I noticed under the edge of the fountain a tiny sack of spider eggs just hatching. Hundreds of tiny spiders were making their way to the edge of the concrete. They were jumping off and taking flight. Flying away on the breeze.

"Ahh look, girls! Look at this!" As I spoke to them, I thought, *No more.* Silently I said, *Trauma, you no longer have a home in my spirit. You are no longer nourished in the cracks and crevices of my lived story within my body. No more spiders living off the pain.*

I had remembered, finally. I had remembered and faced the truth of what I had been carrying. I faced the history and ancestral trauma that had been handed down from my great elders for eons. I knew from that day forward that I would not carry that onward to my girls or out into the world anymore. Certainly not in the same way. I know I will have new lessons and histories to uncover. But this tragic and beautiful and painful part of me can fly away. The spiders were finally free to fly to a new home, someplace else.

I looked at my girls, and I knew that their lives would change forever in that moment. All from the bravery of little Lu. Healing her past so that I no longer had to carry those memories in my being was freeing to us all.

I looked up, and a bluebird perched on the tree next me. I swear it tilted its head and winked at me.

Then I heard my husband, Marcus, calling my name.

I called out in return, "I'm here! We're here!"

He gathered us up in his arms and said, "There you are! I see you!"

"Yes, yes, here I am! I am here!"

I am here.

Turning my face to the sun, I looked up into the clouds. I saw Kelda sitting on a cloud that looked a little something like a tree. Kelda let out a big sigh and laughed. She was sitting on a celestial tree branch that seemed to be firmly rooted in the stars. Kelda was not alone.

"Kelda?"

"Yes, my dear?"

"Do you think she knew I had anything to do with her healing?"

"No, Julia, However, I am sure she will come to know in time. That must have been hard for you."

"It was my honor."

RESOURCES

If you or someone you know is in crisis, there are many resources that can help. These hotlines and organizations are free and available to anyone who is struggling. This is not a complete list of resources, but it is a good start.

Hotlines in the United States

Emergency: 911

Suicide and Crisis Hotline: 988
National Suicide Prevention Lifeline: 1-800-273-TALK (8255)
text HOME or DESERVE to 741-741 or visit **https://speakingof-suicide.com/resources** for additional resources. **1-800-SUICIDE (800-784-2433)**

The Substance Abuse and Mental Health Services Administration has a 24/7 National Helpline for individuals with substance abuse issues and their family members. The hotline, which offers assistance in English and Spanish, can be reached at **1-800-662-HELP (4357)**. To find behavioral health treatment services, visit **https://findtreatment.samhsa.gov/**.

The National Eating Disorders Association runs a helpline offering support, resources, and treatment options. Call or text **1-800-931-2237** during select hours or **text NEDA to 741741** at any hour in a crisis. For more information about eating disorders, visit **https://nationaleatingdisorders.org.**

National Domestic Violence Hotline: 1-800-799-7233 or go to **www.thehotline.org** for anonymous, confidential online chats, available in English and Spanish. Individual states often have their own domestic violence hotlines as well.

National Sexual Assault Telephone Hotline: 1-800-656-4673. The hotline, run by the **Rape, Abuse & Incest National Network (RAINN),** can put you in contact with your local rape crisis center. You can also access RAINN's online chat service at **https://www.rainn.org/get-help.**

Lifeline Crisis Chat: https://suicidepreventionlifeline.org/chat/ (Online live messaging)

Self-Harm Hotline: 1-800-DONT-CUT (1-800-366-8288), https://selfinjury.com

Planned Parenthood Hotline: 1-800-230-PLAN (7526)

GLBT National Hotline: 1-888-843-4564

TREVOR Project LGBTQ Crisis Hotline: 1-866-488-7386. Live chat on their website: **https://www.thetrevorproject.org/get-help/** or **text START to 678-678**

TransLifeline: 1-877-565-8860 and **https://www.translifeline.org**

Therapist Finder: To Find a therapist in your area, go to **https://www.psychologytoday.com.**

ACKNOWLEDGMENTS

Truth be told, a lot of this book was written in my bathtub. I began this book while I was on a sabbatical from my private practice as a psychotherapist. I contracted Lyme Disease and was in constant pain. The only place that felt good was my bathtub, filled to the rim with added salt and minerals. Therefore, I would like to thank water for saving me. Kelda said many times throughout Wilumina's journey, "Water is the Way." I am only now understanding how true that statement is. Water has been the way. Whether it was the water I gratefully drank while writing, or the water in my bathtub, or in my tears, or the actual rolling Pacific Ocean, water has held me and rocked me and guided me through this amazing experience.

Dr. Tererai Trent, thank you for inspiring me to begin. Sharing your own story so bravely showed me that I too could achieve my dreams. Tinogona! It IS achievable!

In the early days of writing, I have Azul Terronez to thank you for helping me imagine all the characters and bring them to life. Being a part of your writers' group really helped me to see I was not alone and made the process of conceptualization a joy! Tierra Destiny Reid, thank you for taking my writings from a document of unrelated stories to the beginnings of what was to become my biggest dream come true.

Melanie Gorman your support and guidance has been invaluable. You came in and saved the day when I was feeling hopeless about this story ever seeing the light of day. Thank you for your thoughtful edits and suggestions on how to improve the storyline. You've been able to wrangle me in and create a cohesive plan when all I saw was pandemonium and sparkles.

Elizabeth and Chris Day, you also came in at the final hour with editing, fantastic insights and careful attention to detail. You have brought your own special magic to this book, and it is a deep honor for me to be a part of it.

Brianna Cillessen, thank you for understanding how my creative mind works and channeling my energy into the right direction and camera lens. Your own creativity, brilliant practicality and style have been invaluable for me. And that hubby of yours, Thomas Faverty, thank you for bringing us all together through your love of skateboarding and mad camera skills.

Jennifer S. Wilkov, thank you for bringing the concept and image of *Wilumina and the Well* from the computer to something I could hold in my hands. Simply miraculous! Thank you!

I want to specifically thank my clients. You have been an inspiration to me. There is a part of each of you in Wilumina. (I wish I could name you personally but that would be a big HIPAA violation.) You courageously invited me into your lives and trusted me with your darkest secrets and your greatest joys. To be able to witness your healing and your growth over the years has been one of my great honors. You have shown me in a myriad of ways what grace, for-giveness and strength looks and feels like. I deeply bow to you.

A small circle of unmatchable friends helped me in countless ways. Thank you to those who contributed to the creation and completion of this book. You assisted me in so many ways from holding space for me to dream this book into existence, to char-acter names or to cover design suggestions, and all the things in between. I am deeply humbled by the encouragement and enthu-siasm you have shown me.

Speaking of safety and compassion, thank you to each of my first readers. Thank you for your solid advice, humor, magical light, as well as your excel spreadsheet and editing skills. You each showed me in a thousand ways that I had something special and to keep moving forward. Step by step, you said, "We've got this!" Your love and friendship took *Wilumina and the Well* from "my book" to "our book".

To my family, only you can understand what it took to put this story to paper. May this book offer healing and guidance for us all. My nieces and nephews, may you go forth and create families based in collective trust, love, and safety. Since the inception of *Wilumina and the Well* I have been in awe many times of our family's collective capacity for healing. Dad when you asked for the gift of healing for your 80th birthday, you set in motion an open and honest conversation that blew all our hearts wide open. Every beat of your heart has been a sacred blessing. Thank you for all your encouragement, cartoons, and articles about how to be a writer. Thank you for loving books. My sissy, Becky Brewer, thank you for the nights you snuck into my baby crib to quiet my cries. You heard me, you saw me (even way back then) and that has made all the difference for me. My Brodda, Tim Maddox, thank you for forgiving me for being such a mean girl. Thank you for loving me and healing with me and accepting me with open arms. Thank you, Shawn Stewart-Maddox, our friendship, and sisterhood have been nothing short of an answered prayer for me and for our family. Uncle Larry and Aunt Joy, you have been the loving wisdom keepers of our family, for that, I am eternally grateful.

My daughters, Emma, and Charlotte, you have blessed me with your love and your light from day one and even before. You continue to teach me the true meaning of "Nothing but Love!" Because of you, I know how to love with an open heart. I feel blessed beyond measure that you chose me to be your mama. Maya and Nina, you are the best gift your dad ever gave me. You are the best parts of him. Thank you for pushing me and encouraging me though your own courageous lives to be, not only a better mom, but a better human.

My Walter, my love, you'll always be my North Star. Thank you for helping me find my way home and back to you. "I see the doorways of a thousand churches in your eyes." Without you, none of this book would be possible.

About Jennifer Dawn Maddox, LCSW, MASM

 As the owner of a private psychotherapy / coaching practice, Jennifer believes that with mindfulness, grit, a bit of magic and a healthy dose of humor, one can accomplish a deep and meaningful life. She combines her clinical knowledge and practices with conscious breathwork and psychedelic-assisted psychotherapy for transformative client-centered healing, bringing a sense of spirituality and joy to her clients.

Jennifer holds two master's degrees, a Clinical Social Work degree from the University of Denver's Graduate School of Social Work and a second master's degree in Specialized Ministry from Iliff School of Theology. In 2021, Jennifer trained with the Multidisciplinary Association of Psychedelic Studies (MAPS) for MDMA Assisted Psychotherapy and is also certified in Psychedelic Somatic Interactive Psychotherapy. In addition to her clinical training, Jennifer is a certified as a Conscious Breathwork facilitator and a Reiki Master. She is an avid student of meditation, plant medicines, yoga, and non-ordinary states of consciousness.

Jennifer lives in Denver Colorado and in Todos Santos, Baja California Mexico with her partner Walter. None of the above compares to her experience as a mother of two beautiful daughters by birth and two more by marriage. Jennifer is dedicated to making the world, or at least her parts of the world, wherever they may be, just a little more beautiful than when she arrived.

 www.jenniferdmaddox.com

 @jenniferdawnmaddox

 @JenniferDMaddoxLCSW